DEMENTIA CAREGIVER'S GUIDE

Compassionate Navigation Through Healthcare,
Building Support Networks, Embracing Self-Care, and
Providing Guidance for the Final Journey

VIVIAN HART

Contents

Introduction

The day my mother looked at me and asked, "Who are you?" was the day everything changed. That simple question, uttered with genuine curiosity and no recognition in her eyes, marked the beginning of our journey into the world of dementia caregiving. Like many caregivers, I faced a whirlwind of emotions—grief, confusion, frustration, and a deep sense of love that kept me moving forward. It didn't take long to realize that caregiving would be one of the most challenging roles I would ever take on, requiring me to become an advocate, a researcher, a nurse, and, above all, a source of steady comfort.

Dementia caregiving is not a role anyone volunteers for, but it is a role many step into out of love and necessity. This book was born out of my experiences and those of countless others who have faced similar challenges. It is a tribute to the resilience, compassion, and ingenuity of caregivers everywhere. I understand the sleepless nights, the endless questions, and the overwhelming need for guidance and support because I've been there. I know the heartbreak of watching someone you love slip away and the small victories that bring moments of joy amidst the struggle.

This book is here to serve as a beacon of hope and a trusted companion. Its purpose is to provide a comprehensive, empathetic guide to navigating dementia caregiving. With actionable strategies, emotional support, and deep insights, it is designed to equip caregivers with the tools they need to manage the practical aspects of caregiving while also addressing their emotional and psychological well-being. More than just a manual, this book is an invitation to connect—with your loved one, with other caregivers, and with yourself.

If you are reading this, you are likely a caregiver, or about to become one, seeking clarity in an often overwhelming world. Whether you are just beginning this journey or are deep into the caregiving process, this book is tailored specifically for you. It offers practical advice for daily care, strategies for managing difficult moments, and a roadmap for navigating the complex systems of healthcare, legal planning, and financial management. It also delves into the emotional and psychological aspects of caregiving, ensuring that your well-being is not overlooked.

The book is structured to guide you through every stage of the caregiving journey. It begins with an overview of dementia, offering a solid foundation of understanding. From there, it provides practical caregiving strategies, emotional support for caregivers, and tools for managing legal and financial challenges. Later chapters address advanced care planning and offer guidance for finding closure and moving forward after caregiving. Each chapter builds on the last, providing a comprehensive and cohesive resource to support you at every step.

Throughout this book, you will find professional recommendations from healthcare experts, alongside stories from real caregivers who have generously shared their experiences. These stories are windows into the lives of others who have walked this path, offering lessons, inspiration, and solidarity.

At its heart, this book also prioritizes self-care. You cannot pour from an empty cup, and your health, happiness, and resilience are essential —not only for you but also for your ability to provide the best care possible. You will find strategies and resources throughout the book dedicated to helping you maintain your own well-being while navigating the demands of caregiving.

Finally, this book is an invitation to join a community of caregivers. You are not alone. Whether you connect with others through support groups, online forums, or the stories within these pages, you are part of a larger network of individuals who share in your challenges and celebrate your victories.

While the road ahead may be difficult, you are not walking it alone. This book will equip you with the knowledge, strategies, and support you need to navigate dementia caregiving with confidence. More than anything, I hope it will remind you that you are stronger than you think, that your role is invaluable, and that even in the hardest moments, there is love, hope, and purpose. Let this be the beginning of a journey where, together, we find strength, resilience, and meaning. Welcome.

ONE

Demystifying Dementia

The Nature of Dementia: Beyond Memory Loss

Dementia is often misunderstood as simply a condition of memory loss, a characterization that oversimplifies its profound and multifaceted nature. While forgetfulness is one hallmark, dementia encompasses a wide spectrum of symptoms that affect thinking, social abilities, and daily functioning. Understanding the true nature of dementia is crucial for caregivers, enabling them to provide more effective and compassionate support.

At its core, dementia is a syndrome—a collection of symptoms caused by disorders that affect the brain. It is not a single disease but a term that describes a range of cognitive impairments severe enough to interfere with daily life. Alzheimer's disease is the most common cause, accounting for 60–80% of dementia cases, but other forms include vascular dementia, frontotemporal dementia, and Lewy body dementia, each with its own patterns and challenges. Regardless of the cause, dementia fundamentally alters how a person processes and interacts with the world.

The symptoms of dementia extend far beyond memory loss, affecting nearly every aspect of cognition and function. Language, for instance, can be significantly impaired. Individuals may struggle to find the right words, follow conversations, or express themselves clearly. Problem-solving and decision-making abilities also deteriorate, making it difficult for someone to manage finances, navigate daily tasks, or respond to unforeseen challenges. In some forms of dementia, physical abilities are affected as well, resulting in issues like impaired motor coordination or difficulty swallowing. Behavioral changes—such as agitation, apathy, or repetitive actions—further complicate the condition and its management.

Recognizing early symptoms of dementia is critical, especially those unrelated to memory. Early signs might include subtle changes in behavior, difficulty with planning or organizing, or challenges in interpreting visual or spatial information. For instance, someone might struggle to judge distances while driving or find it increasingly hard to follow a recipe they've used for years. These non-memory-related symptoms often emerge before noticeable forgetfulness, serving as red flags that should not be ignored.

Timely recognition of these symptoms allows for earlier intervention, which can significantly improve quality of life for both the individual and their caregivers. Early diagnosis enables access to treatments that may slow progression, support systems that enhance daily functioning, and resources that prepare families for the journey ahead. It also provides the person with dementia an opportunity to participate in planning their care, voicing their preferences while they are still able.

The cognitive and behavioral changes brought by dementia pose profound challenges to a person's sense of self. As abilities diminish, the individual may feel a growing disconnection from their identity, relationships, and the roles they once held. For example, a former teacher who prided themselves on their communication skills may struggle with finding words, leading to frustration and a sense of loss. These changes not only affect how they see themselves but also how others perceive and interact with them.

For caregivers, understanding the impact of dementia on personhood is essential. Symptoms like irritability or withdrawal are not just frustrating behaviors; they are expressions of a person grappling with a shifting sense of identity. Recognizing this fosters empathy and allows caregivers to focus on preserving the individual's dignity, even as dementia reshapes their abilities.

Dementia is not merely about what is lost—it is about finding ways to adapt, connect, and support those living with it. By understanding dementia as more than memory loss, caregivers can approach the condition with greater compassion and readiness. They can help maintain their loved one's sense of self, even in the face of profound changes, and create a caregiving environment that prioritizes dignity and connection. This chapter lays the foundation for that understanding, offering a lens through which to see dementia not as a monolith, but as a complex and deeply human condition.

Understanding Different Types of Dementia

Dementia is not a singular condition but a broad term encompassing several distinct types, each with unique causes, symptoms, and progression patterns. Recognizing these differences is critical for caregivers, as it informs diagnosis, treatment, and care strategies tailored to the individual's needs. While Alzheimer's disease is the most well-known, other types—vascular dementia, Lewy body dementia, and frontotemporal dementia—add layers of complexity to the caregiving journey.

Alzheimer's disease is the most common form of dementia, accounting for 60–80% of cases. It is characterized by memory loss, confusion, difficulty with language, and disorientation. In its early stages, individuals may struggle to recall recent events or conversations, while later stages bring significant impairments in cognitive function, behavior, and physical abilities. Alzheimer's is a progressive disease, typically advancing over several years, with hallmark changes in the brain, such as the buildup of amyloid plaques and tau tangles.

Vascular dementia, the second most common type, results from reduced blood flow to the brain, often caused by strokes or other vascular conditions. Its symptoms can vary widely depending on the areas of the brain affected, but they often include impaired judgment, difficulty with problem-solving, and slowed thinking. Unlike the steady progression of Alzheimer's, vascular dementia may follow a stepwise decline, with symptoms worsening suddenly after additional strokes or vascular events.

Lewy body dementia is marked by the presence of abnormal protein deposits in the brain known as Lewy bodies. This type of dementia is often associated with pronounced visual hallucinations, fluctuations in attention or alertness, and symptoms similar to Parkinson's disease, such as tremors and rigidity. Caregivers of individuals with Lewy body dementia often face unique challenges due to the unpredictable nature of these symptoms, which can vary widely from day to day.

Frontotemporal dementia primarily affects the frontal and temporal lobes of the brain, which control personality, behavior, and language. Unlike Alzheimer's, memory loss is not typically an early symptom. Instead, individuals may experience dramatic changes in personality, a loss of social inhibitions, or difficulty with language and comprehension. This form of dementia often begins at a younger age than others, with many cases diagnosed in people in their 40s or 50s.

Each type of dementia presents unique symptoms and progression patterns, making accurate diagnosis a cornerstone of effective care. However, diagnosing the specific type of dementia can be challenging. Symptoms often overlap, and conditions like depression, delirium, or medication side effects can mimic dementia. Additionally, some individuals may have mixed dementia, a combination of two or more types, such as Alzheimer's and vascular dementia, further complicating diagnosis. Neurologists and geriatric specialists rely on a combination of medical history, cognitive tests, imaging, and biomarkers to pinpoint the underlying cause.

Accurate diagnosis is crucial not only for understanding the disease but also for tailoring caregiving strategies. Knowing the specific type of dementia enables caregivers and healthcare providers to anticipate progression patterns, manage symptoms more effectively, and provide targeted interventions. For instance, caregivers of individuals with vascular dementia may focus on managing cardiovascular health to prevent further decline, while those supporting someone with Lewy body dementia may need to address hallucinations and motor symptoms.

Treatment approaches also vary depending on the type of dementia. While no cure exists for most forms of dementia, medications like cholinesterase inhibitors and memantine may help manage cognitive symptoms in Alzheimer's and Lewy body dementia. Non-pharmacological interventions, such as cognitive therapies, physical activity, and structured routines, are equally important across all types. For frontotemporal dementia, where behavior changes are prominent, strategies for managing social and emotional symptoms become a key focus.

Understanding the specific type of dementia opens the door to more personalized care, enabling caregivers to navigate challenges with greater confidence and empathy. Each diagnosis carries unique implications, but it also provides clarity, empowering caregivers to support their loved ones in ways that honor their individuality and needs.

Recognizing the Early Signs of Dementia

Dementia often begins with subtle changes that are easy to overlook or dismiss as normal aging. These early signs, though minor at first, can signal the onset of a progressive condition that affects memory, thinking, and behavior. Recognizing these initial symptoms is a vital step toward early intervention, better management, and improved quality of life for both the individual and their caregivers.

The early stages of dementia often manifest as small disruptions in daily life. A loved one may experience mild memory lapses, such as forgetting appointments or misplacing items. These occasional slips might initially seem unremarkable, especially in older adults. However, when memory problems start to interfere with routine tasks or conversations—such as repeatedly asking the same question or struggling to recall recent events—it may indicate the early stages of dementia.

Other early signs include changes in mood or personality. Someone who was once outgoing and energetic may become withdrawn or apathetic. Conversely, individuals might exhibit heightened irritability or anxiety, reacting strongly to minor frustrations. These emotional shifts often reflect the growing difficulty in processing and adapting to changes in cognitive function. Difficulty with familiar tasks, such as balancing a checkbook, cooking a favorite recipe, or using a device they've always managed with ease, is another hallmark of early dementia.

Language difficulties can also emerge in subtle ways. A person may have trouble finding the right words during conversations or repeat themselves frequently. They might struggle to follow a conversation or lose their train of thought mid-sentence. Spatial awareness and problem-solving skills may also decline, leading to challenges like navigating once-familiar routes or organizing their daily schedule.

Recognizing these symptoms early is crucial for timely detection and diagnosis. Early detection allows individuals and their families to access resources, begin medical treatments that may slow disease progression, and plan for the future while the individual is still able to participate in decision-making. For example, treatments like cholinesterase inhibitors may be most effective in the early stages of Alzheimer's, and non-medical interventions such as cognitive therapies can help preserve function and independence.

The importance of early detection extends beyond medical treatment. Understanding what is happening empowers families to approach the situation with empathy and preparedness. It reduces the uncertainty and frustration that often accompany unexplained changes in behavior or cognition, allowing caregivers to adapt their expectations and strategies.

Knowing when to seek professional help can make all the difference. If you notice persistent memory issues, confusion, or changes in behavior that interfere with daily life, it's time to consult a healthcare provider. A general practitioner can conduct initial evaluations and refer the individual to a specialist, such as a neurologist or geriatric psychiatrist, for further testing. Diagnostic processes may include cognitive assessments, medical history reviews, and brain imaging to rule out other conditions, such as depression or vitamin deficiencies, that can mimic dementia.

Caregivers who identify early signs of dementia in their loved ones often face a mix of emotions—concern for their loved one's well-being, fear about the future, and uncertainty about how to proceed. It's essential to seek support during this time. Local support groups, national organizations like the Alzheimer's Association (*alz.org*), and online forums can provide caregivers with information, guidance, and a sense of community. Educational workshops or counseling services specifically geared toward early-stage caregiving can also equip families with the tools they need to navigate this phase.

Recognizing the early signs of dementia is the beginning of a long and challenging journey, but it is also a step toward empowerment and preparation. By acting on these early indicators, caregivers and families can access the resources and support needed to provide compassionate, informed care. Early detection paves the way for a more manageable and intentional approach to the challenges ahead, fostering a sense of hope and control in the face of an uncertain future.

The Progression of Dementia: What to Expect

Dementia is a progressive condition, which means it worsens over time. While every individual's journey is unique, the progression typically follows a general pattern of three stages: early (mild), middle (moderate), and late (severe). Understanding these stages can help caregivers anticipate changes, adapt care strategies, and prepare for emotional and physical demands.

In the early stage of dementia, symptoms are mild and may even go unnoticed for some time. Memory lapses are often the first noticeable sign, such as forgetting recent conversations, misplacing items, or struggling to recall names. However, these lapses usually don't interfere significantly with daily life. Your loved one may still function independently but need occasional reminders or support with more complex tasks, like managing finances or following a recipe.

Emotionally, this stage can be difficult for both the person with dementia and their caregivers. Your loved one may feel frustrated or embarrassed by their lapses, leading to withdrawal from social activities. Anxiety and depression are also common as they become more aware of their limitations. For caregivers, this stage is an opportunity to establish routines, create memory aids, and begin planning for future care while your loved one can still participate in decisions.

As dementia progresses into the middle stage, symptoms become more pronounced and begin to interfere with daily life. Memory loss deepens, and your loved one may struggle to recognize familiar faces, recall important events, or navigate familiar environments. Communication becomes increasingly difficult as language skills decline, leading to fragmented or repetitive conversations. They may also need help with daily tasks like dressing, bathing, or preparing meals.

Behavioral changes often become more noticeable in the middle stage. Your loved one might exhibit confusion, agitation, or aggression, particularly in unfamiliar or overwhelming situations. Paranoia, delusions, and hallucinations can also emerge, making caregiving more challenging. For example, they may accuse you of hiding their belongings or believe they are in a different time or place. Sleep disturbances, including restlessness and sundowning (increased confusion in the evening), are common during this stage.

The middle stage places significant demands on caregivers. You may need to provide constant supervision to ensure your loved one's safety, especially if they are prone to wandering or accidents. This is also the time to involve a broader support network, whether through family, friends, or professional caregiving services. Sharing the responsibilities can help alleviate the emotional and physical strain on primary caregivers.

In the late stage of dementia, symptoms are severe, and your loved one becomes fully dependent on others for care. They may lose the ability to communicate verbally, recognize even close family members, or perform basic motor functions. Swallowing difficulties and weight loss are common, as are increased vulnerability to infections like pneumonia. At this stage, the focus shifts to providing comfort and maintaining dignity.

While the late stage is emotionally challenging, it also offers opportunities for connection in different ways. Even if verbal communication is no longer possible, your loved one may still respond to touch, music, or familiar voices. Simple acts like holding their hand, playing calming music, or sitting quietly together can provide reassurance and a sense of connection.

Throughout all stages, the progression of dementia is rarely linear. Symptoms may fluctuate, with good days and bad days. These inconsistencies can be confusing and emotionally draining, but they are a natural part of the disease. Caregivers must remain flexible, adjusting their approach as needs change.

Understanding the progression of dementia also helps caregivers plan for the future. This includes making decisions about long-term care options, financial planning, and end-of-life care. While these conversations are difficult, having plans in place reduces stress and ensures that your loved one's preferences are respected.

Dementia's progression can feel relentless, but it also presents opportunities for growth, resilience, and connection. By understanding the stages and preparing for the challenges ahead, caregivers can navigate this journey compassionately, ensuring their loved ones receive the care and support they need.

Dementia's Impact on the Brain: A Caregiver's Guide

Dementia is not just a condition of forgetfulness; it is a profound neurological disorder that alters the physical structure and function of the brain. For caregivers, understanding the underlying brain changes that drive dementia's symptoms can provide valuable insights into the disease and foster greater empathy and patience in care. By connecting the dots between brain function and behavior, caregivers can approach their role with enhanced understanding and compassion.

At its core, dementia is caused by damage to brain cells and the connections between them. This damage disrupts communication pathways within the brain, impairing its ability to process, store, and retrieve information. In conditions like Alzheimer's disease, abnormal proteins, such as amyloid plaques and tau tangles, accumulate in the brain, leading to widespread cell death. In vascular dementia, reduced blood flow deprives brain cells of oxygen and nutrients, causing localized damage. Regardless of the specific cause, these neurological changes compromise the brain's ability to perform essential functions.

The symptoms of dementia can often be traced to specific areas of the brain that are affected. For instance, the hippocampus, responsible for forming and storing new memories, is one of the first areas to show damage in Alzheimer's disease, explaining why memory loss is a hallmark early symptom. Damage to the frontal lobes, which govern decision-making, behavior, and social skills, can lead to impulsivity, difficulty planning, or personality changes, as seen in frontotemporal dementia. The occipital lobe, which processes visual information, may be affected in certain cases, leading to visual misperceptions or hallucinations, as is common in Lewy body dementia. Recognizing these connections helps caregivers better understand the "why" behind their loved one's behaviors and challenges.

Despite the progressive nature of dementia, the brain retains some capacity for adaptability, known as neuroplasticity. Neuroplasticity refers to the brain's ability to reorganize itself by forming new connections between neurons. While this capacity is limited in the context of dementia, certain activities can stimulate remaining neural pathways and enhance quality of life. Engaging individuals in cognitive exercises, physical activity, and meaningful social interactions has been shown to help preserve brain function and delay cognitive decline to some extent. For example, playing music, solving puzzles, or practicing routines that rely on long-term memory may tap into preserved brain areas, fostering engagement and emotional connection.

Equipping caregivers with a deeper understanding of the brain changes associated with dementia transforms caregiving from a series of tasks into a compassionate and informed practice. Knowing that repeated questions or difficulty following a conversation stem from brain cell damage—not willfulness or inattention—helps caregivers approach these moments with patience rather than frustration. Understanding how the brain's deterioration affects emotions, behavior, and perception enables caregivers to tailor their strategies and responses, enhancing their loved one's sense of safety and dignity.

This educational insight empowers caregivers to develop empathy not just for the individual but also for themselves. Recognizing that dementia is a neurological condition beyond anyone's control can ease feelings of guilt or inadequacy, replacing them with a sense of purpose and resilience. Caregiving becomes less about "fixing" symptoms and more about navigating them with creativity and compassion, focusing on maintaining connection and quality of life.

As caregivers gain knowledge about the brain and its role in dementia, they prepare to embark on the next phase of their journey: managing the emotional impact of the disease. Understanding the science behind dementia lays a foundation for addressing its emotional complexities, both for the individual and the caregiver. The next chapter, delves into the emotional terrain of caregiving, offering guidance on navigating the grief, joy, and resilience that define this path.

TWO

The Emotional Journey of Dementia

Navigating the Emotional Stages of Dementia for Caregivers

Caregiving for someone with dementia is as much an emotional journey as it is a practical one. It is an experience filled with an ever-shifting range of emotions, from moments of love and connection to times of frustration and grief. Navigating this emotional rollercoaster is one of the most challenging yet transformative aspects of caregiving, and understanding its complexities can help caregivers approach their role with greater compassion and resilience.

The emotional journey often begins with denial, especially in the early stages of dementia. A loved one's forgetfulness or behavioral changes may be dismissed as normal aging, leading caregivers to avoid confronting the possibility of a serious condition. As the signs become more evident, denial may give way to confusion or frustration. Caregivers may feel overwhelmed by the demands of caregiving or struggle to understand why their loved one is acting in unfamiliar ways. Anger is another common emotion, often directed at the disease itself, at the lack of external support, or even, in fleeting moments, at the person with dementia. These feelings are natural and part of the process of coming to terms with the reality of the situation.

Over time, many caregivers experience a profound sense of sadness or grief. This grief, often described as anticipatory grief, arises as they mourn the gradual loss of the person they once knew, even as they continue to care for them. This phase can feel particularly isolating, as the caregiver is experiencing loss while their loved one is still physically present. Balancing these emotions with moments of connection—when a familiar laugh or smile reminds the caregiver of their shared bond—can create a poignant mix of sorrow and joy.

It is important to understand that unlike the clinical stages of dementia, the emotional stages caregivers experience are not linear. A day that begins with acceptance and calm may spiral into frustration and sadness by evening. Caregivers may feel as though they are progressing emotionally, only to find themselves revisiting feelings of anger or denial during particularly difficult moments. This variability is entirely normal and reflects the dynamic nature of caregiving. The key is to allow these emotions to surface without judgment, recognizing that each feeling is valid and part of the journey.

Seeking emotional support is crucial for navigating these stages. Connecting with others who understand the caregiver's experience can provide much-needed validation and encouragement. Support groups, whether in person or online, offer a space to share stories, vent frustrations, and exchange advice. Therapy or counseling can also be immensely helpful, providing caregivers with tools to process complex emotions and develop coping strategies. Online communities, forums, and social media groups tailored to dementia caregivers create opportunities for connection even for those unable to leave home due to caregiving responsibilities.

Maintaining personal well-being is essential to sustain caregivers emotionally and mentally. Self-care often takes a backseat to caregiving duties, but neglecting one's own needs can lead to burnout, depression, or physical illness. Simple strategies, such as setting aside time for exercise, pursuing hobbies, or even taking short breaks throughout the day, can recharge emotional reserves. Mindfulness techniques, such as meditation or breathing exercises, can help caregivers stay grounded during moments of stress. Seeking respite care, whether for an afternoon or a weekend, provides the space needed to rest and reset.

Caregiving is an act of profound love and dedication, but it is also one of immense emotional complexity. By acknowledging and addressing the full range of emotions that accompany this role, caregivers can approach their journey with greater resilience and self-compassion.

Dealing with Grief and Loss Before the End

Grief is often thought of as something that happens after a loved one passes away, but for caregivers of individuals with dementia, grief often begins much earlier. This anticipatory grief arises as caregivers mourn the gradual loss of the person their loved one once was, even while they are still physically present. Dealing with this type of grief can be one of the most emotionally challenging aspects of caregiving, yet it also offers an opportunity to adapt, reflect, and find new ways to connect.

Anticipatory grief is a natural response to the changes brought by dementia. Caregivers often feel they are losing pieces of their loved one's identity as memory fades, behaviors shift, and the ability to communicate diminishes. For example, a parent who was once a pillar of wisdom may now struggle to recognize their own child. A partner who shared a lifetime of memories may no longer recall the relationship's most significant moments. This loss of shared history and connection can create a profound sense of sadness and longing.

Coping with anticipatory grief requires acknowledging and embracing these feelings without judgment. It is okay to feel sadness, frustration, or even anger at the situation. These emotions do not diminish the love and care you provide; they are a testament to the depth of your bond. Journaling can be a helpful outlet for processing these emotions, allowing caregivers to reflect on their journey and express feelings they may struggle to share aloud. Support groups and therapy also provide a safe space to explore grief and find comfort among others who understand the unique challenges of dementia caregiving.

Another important coping mechanism is focusing on the aspects of the relationship that remain. While dementia changes many things, it does not erase the capacity for meaningful connection. Look for moments of joy, such as a shared smile, a familiar song that sparks recognition, or the warmth of holding hands. These moments, though fleeting, can be deeply fulfilling and provide a reminder that the essence of your loved one is still present in many ways.

It's essential to normalize feelings of loss and affirm that it is okay to grieve for someone who is still alive. Caregivers often experience guilt for feeling sadness or for longing for the person their loved one used to be. Understanding that these feelings are a natural part of anticipatory grief can help ease this guilt. Grieving while caregiving does not mean giving up hope or love; it is a way of processing the profound changes dementia brings.

As dementia progresses, caregivers may find comfort in creating a new kind of relationship with their loved one. This involves adapting to who the person is in the present rather than focusing solely on who they were in the past. For example, instead of engaging in complex conversations that may no longer be possible, caregivers can share in simpler activities like listening to music, looking through old photos, or enjoying quiet moments together. These interactions nurture a bond that transcends the losses and creates a sense of connection rooted in the present.

Building a new relationship also means redefining expectations and finding new ways to communicate. Non-verbal interactions, such as touch, facial expressions, or tone of voice, become increasingly important as verbal communication becomes more difficult. Patience, flexibility, and creativity are key to maintaining a meaningful connection as dementia progresses.

Anticipatory grief is a difficult but natural part of the caregiving journey. By acknowledging these feelings, seeking support, and embracing the evolving nature of the relationship, caregivers can navigate this complex emotional terrain with compassion and resilience.

The Changing Dynamics of Relationships

One of the most profound challenges of dementia caregiving is the shifting dynamics of the relationship between the caregiver and their loved one. Spouses become caregivers, children take on parental roles, and the once-familiar ways of connecting are altered by the disease. Navigating these changes with patience, understanding, and adaptability is essential for maintaining a sense of closeness and mutual respect throughout the journey.

The transition from spouse or child to caregiver represents a fundamental role reversal that can be emotionally difficult. A husband or wife who once relied on their partner for companionship and shared decision-making may now find themselves managing every aspect of their loved one's care. Similarly, children may grapple with stepping into a parental role for the very person who raised them. This shift can evoke a mix of emotions, including sadness for the loss of the previous dynamic, resentment over the added responsibilities, and guilt for struggling with these feelings.

Acknowledging these emotions is the first step in adapting to the new reality. It's important to allow yourself to mourn the loss of the relationship as it was, even as you commit to supporting your loved one in their current needs. Seeking support from peers or professionals can provide a space to process these changes and find validation in your experience.

Communication is another area profoundly affected by dementia, often leading to frustration and feelings of disconnection. As cognitive decline progresses, verbal communication may become fragmented or inconsistent, with your loved one struggling to find words, follow conversations, or respond appropriately. To maintain meaningful interaction, focus on simplifying communication. Speak clearly, use short sentences, and allow time for your loved one to process and respond. Non-verbal cues, such as eye contact, tone of voice, and gentle touch, become increasingly important as words become harder to find. These simple gestures convey care and understanding, even when verbal exchanges are limited.

Preserving dignity and respect is paramount as dementia progresses and your loved one becomes increasingly dependent on your support. It can be easy to unintentionally infantilize someone with dementia when assisting with tasks like dressing or eating, but it's crucial to approach caregiving in a way that affirms their sense of self. Whenever possible, involve them in decision-making, offer choices, and encourage independence in activities they can still manage. For example, if choosing an outfit for the day becomes overwhelming, present two options instead of a full wardrobe, empowering them to make the final selection.

Privacy and autonomy are also key aspects of maintaining dignity. Respect their personal space during caregiving activities and be mindful of how care is delivered, especially in front of others. If they need assistance with sensitive tasks, such as bathing, create an environment that feels safe and private, reinforcing their sense of respect and trust.

Adjusting expectations of the relationship is another important step in adapting to dementia's impact. The dynamic will inevitably change, but this does not mean the bond must weaken. Instead, caregivers can focus on finding new ways to connect that reflect the reality of the present. For example, if deep conversations are no longer possible, shared activities like listening to music, enjoying nature, or looking at old photos can foster connection and joy. These moments emphasize the emotional bond rather than the cognitive abilities that may have been lost.

Learning to cherish small victories and moments of recognition, even when they are fleeting, helps create positive experiences within the new framework of the relationship. Understanding that your loved one's responses and behaviors are shaped by the disease, not by intent, can also reduce frustration and foster empathy.

The changing dynamics of relationships in dementia caregiving require ongoing adjustment, but they also offer opportunities to discover new depths of love and connection. By embracing flexibility, prioritizing dignity, and focusing on the moments that matter, caregivers can preserve the essence of their bond, even as it evolves.

Finding Joy and Connection in the Caregiving Journey

Caregiving for a loved one with dementia is filled with challenges, but it is also interwoven with opportunities for joy and connection. These moments may look different than they once did, but they hold profound value. By focusing on the present, adapting activities, and creating a nurturing environment, caregivers can foster meaningful interactions and strengthen their bond with their loved one.

Celebrating the present is a powerful way to find joy in caregiving. While dementia often feels like a long series of losses, it also offers moments of beauty and connection. A shared laugh over something silly, a quiet moment holding hands, or the spark of recognition in your loved one's eyes—these instances remind caregivers that the essence of their loved one is still present. Instead of dwelling on what has changed, caregivers can focus on what remains, finding gratitude in the here and now.

Adapting activities to suit your loved one's current abilities is another way to cultivate joy and engagement. Many favorite pastimes can be modified to match their evolving needs. For example, if your loved one once enjoyed cooking, involve them in simpler tasks like stirring batter or arranging ingredients. Gardening can be adapted by providing small pots for planting or watering. For those who loved puzzles, choosing ones with fewer pieces or larger designs can make the activity enjoyable again. The key is to tailor the activity to their strengths, ensuring they feel successful and included.

Sensory stimulation is particularly effective in evoking memories and enhancing mood. Music has a remarkable ability to tap into long-term memory, often bringing joy and emotional connection. Playing a favorite song or singing together can elicit smiles and even rekindle lost words. Art projects, like painting or coloring, provide a creative outlet without requiring complex skills. Tactile activities, such as folding soft fabrics, arranging flowers, or feeling different textures, can soothe agitation and spark curiosity. These sensory experiences create opportunities for engagement and communication that transcend cognitive limitations.

The power of routine cannot be overstated in dementia caregiving. Establishing a predictable daily schedule provides structure and comfort for both the caregiver and the individual with dementia.

Familiarity reduces anxiety and helps orient your loved one to their environment, even when memory and cognition are impaired. A consistent routine might include set times for meals, exercise, creative activities, and quiet rest. Within this framework, caregivers can introduce variety through tailored activities and sensory experiences.

Routines also benefit caregivers by providing a sense of control amidst the unpredictability of dementia. Knowing what to expect each day can reduce stress and make caregiving tasks more manageable. Importantly, routines do not need to be rigid; they can incorporate flexibility to accommodate energy levels and moods, ensuring that caregiving remains responsive and compassionate.

Caregivers can also find joy in joining their loved one's world, rather than trying to bring them back into a shared reality. If your loved one believes they are reliving a childhood memory, listen and respond with interest rather than correcting them. These moments of "entering their reality" can create meaningful connections and foster mutual understanding. By focusing on their emotions rather than the accuracy of their perceptions, caregivers can cultivate a sense of trust and security.

Finding joy and connection in everyday moments is not about ignoring the challenges of caregiving but about balancing them with positive experiences that bring fulfillment to both the caregiver and their loved one. By celebrating the present, adapting activities, engaging the senses, and establishing comforting routines, caregivers can create an environment where love and connection thrive.

Coping with the Guilt of Caregiving

Guilt is a deeply personal yet almost universal emotion for caregivers of individuals with dementia. It arises from the immense responsibility of caregiving and the emotional complexity of the role. From feeling like they aren't doing enough to struggling with the need to prioritize their own well-being, caregivers often carry a heavy burden of self-imposed expectations. Understanding caregiver guilt and learning to navigate it is essential for maintaining emotional health and sustaining the ability to provide care.

One common source of guilt is the perception of inadequacy. Caregivers often feel they should be able to handle every challenge perfectly, whether it's responding to difficult behaviors, managing daily tasks, or making decisions about medical care. Each time something doesn't go as planned—if their loved one is upset, if they lose their temper, or if caregiving tasks feel overwhelming—they may find themselves questioning their competence or commitment. These feelings of inadequacy are compounded by the relentless nature of dementia, where every solution seems temporary and the disease's progression feels beyond anyone's control.

Another frequent source of guilt is the internal conflict between caregiving and self-care. Many caregivers feel they must devote all their time and energy to their loved one, seeing any moment spent on themselves as selfish or neglectful. Taking a break, enjoying a hobby, or even expressing frustration can trigger feelings of guilt, as though these actions betray the commitment they've made. Yet neglecting self-care leads to burnout, making it harder to provide the compassionate care their loved one needs.

Guilt also arises in moments of anger or resentment, which are natural responses to the stress and demands of caregiving. Caregivers may feel frustrated with their loved one, especially during difficult behaviors like repetition, wandering, or refusal to cooperate. They may also feel anger at the disease itself or at the situation they find themselves in. When these feelings surface, guilt often follows closely behind, creating a cycle that can feel difficult to break.

Addressing caregiver guilt begins with setting realistic expectations. Caregiving is inherently challenging, and no one can approach it flawlessly. Recognizing this truth allows caregivers to let go of the idea that they must do everything perfectly. Instead, focus on doing the best you can in each moment. Success as a caregiver is not defined by perfection but by the love and effort you bring to your role.

Practicing self-compassion is another critical step in managing guilt. Speak to yourself with the kindness you would extend to a close friend. Remind yourself that caregiving is one of the hardest roles to take on and that feelings of inadequacy or frustration do not diminish your dedication or love. Small acts of self-care—whether it's taking a walk, enjoying a quiet moment with a book, or connecting with a friend—are not indulgences; they are vital to maintaining your own well-being and effectiveness as a caregiver.

Seeking forgiveness from oneself is a powerful process that allows caregivers to let go of guilt and move forward with a lighter heart. Begin by reflecting on the choices you've made and acknowledging the reasons behind them. Understand that every decision was made with the best intentions, even if outcomes were not as you hoped. Embrace the idea that caregiving is about progress, not perfection, and forgive yourself for the inevitable mistakes that come with learning and adapting to this role.

The healing power of self-forgiveness is transformative. By forgiving yourself, you free up emotional energy to focus on the aspects of caregiving that truly matter: connecting with your loved one, adapting to their needs, and finding moments of joy and meaning. Letting go of guilt doesn't mean ignoring challenges—it means approaching them with resilience and self-awareness.

Understanding and addressing caregiver guilt lays the foundation for the practical aspects of caregiving. Emotional work is deeply intertwined with the daily tasks caregivers perform, and finding balance between the two is key to effective care. As we move into the next chapter, *Daily Care Techniques*, we'll focus on actionable strategies for managing the demands of caregiving, from creating routines to ensuring safety and comfort. These tools will empower caregivers to handle the logistical complexities of dementia care with confidence, complementing the emotional resilience developed along the way. Together, these approaches can create a caregiving experience that is both sustainable and deeply fulfilling. Let's step forward into the heart of caregiving with renewed strength and purpose.

THREE

Daily Care Techniques

Creating a Dementia-Friendly Home Environment

A dementia-friendly home environment plays a critical role in enhancing the quality of life for individuals with dementia and their caregivers. By carefully considering safety, navigation, adaptability, and comfort, caregivers can create a space that supports daily living, fosters independence, and reduces stress.

Safety is a primary concern when modifying the home for someone with dementia. Cognitive decline often affects judgment, awareness, and response times, making the risk of accidents higher. Small but meaningful adjustments can minimize hazards and ensure a safer environment. Loose rugs and cables should be removed to prevent tripping, while staircases can be secured with gates or handrails. Ensuring adequate lighting in hallways and stairwells helps reduce disorientation, particularly in the evenings. Cabinets containing hazardous items, such as cleaning supplies or sharp objects, should be locked, and medications stored in secure, clearly labeled containers. Kitchen safety can be improved with stove guards or automatic shutoff devices, reducing the risk of accidents during moments of confusion. Additionally, securing doors that lead to potentially dangerous areas, such as basements or garages, can prevent wandering into unsafe spaces.

Navigation within the home becomes increasingly challenging for individuals with dementia as their condition progresses. Cognitive impairments can make it difficult to remember familiar layouts, identify objects, or find necessary spaces. Clear labels on doors, cabinets, and drawers provide visual guidance and reduce confusion. For instance, labeling the bathroom or marking where everyday items like glasses and plates are stored can promote independence. Strategic use of color and contrast, such as brightly colored tape to highlight doorways or steps, can further improve navigation. Removing visual clutter and maintaining consistent layouts allows for an environment that feels organized and manageable.

As dementia progresses, adapting the living space to accommodate changing needs is essential. Reducing clutter and simplifying room layouts help minimize overstimulation and create a sense of calm. Frequently used items should be kept within reach to avoid frustration or confusion. Furniture should be arranged to provide clear, unobstructed pathways, particularly if mobility becomes an issue. Bathrooms, which can present unique challenges, may require modifications like grab bars near the toilet and shower, non-slip mats, or replacing doorknobs with lever handles. Shower chairs and handheld showerheads can also make bathing safer and more comfortable.

In addition to practicality, the emotional well-being of individuals with dementia can be supported by creating spaces that feel engaging and comforting. Familiar objects like family photos, keepsakes, and favorite books bring a sense of continuity and connection, helping to ground individuals in their surroundings. Sensory items, such as soft blankets, textured cushions, or soothing lights, can provide relaxation and alleviate agitation. Spaces designed for activities—such as a table for puzzles or crafts, a listening station for music, or an area for simple gardening tasks—encourage stimulation and enjoyment, fostering a sense of purpose and accomplishment.

Daily routines can also benefit from a thoughtfully designed home environment. Consistent placement of items and clearly defined spaces help establish familiarity, which reduces anxiety and promotes confidence. Quiet zones where individuals can retreat when overstimulated are equally important, offering a calming environment during challenging moments. Incorporating elements of nature, such as indoor plants or access to a garden, has been shown to improve mood and create a more peaceful atmosphere.

By combining safety measures, thoughtful organization, and personal touches, a dementia-friendly home becomes a space that supports both the individual with dementia and the caregiver. These adjustments not only mitigate risks but also enhance the individual's ability to navigate their surroundings, maintain a sense of independence, and engage with activities that bring them joy.

Nutrition and Hydration: Best Practices for Dementia Care

Maintaining proper nutrition and hydration for someone with dementia is crucial, as their physical and cognitive well-being heavily depend on it. However, dementia often introduces challenges that make mealtime and hydration more complicated. Changes in appetite, difficulty using utensils, forgetfulness about eating or drinking, and even resistance to food or drink are common hurdles that caregivers face. By adopting thoughtful strategies, these challenges can be mitigated to make mealtime an enjoyable and nourishing experience.

Meal planning and preparation take on a new dimension when caring for someone with dementia. Meals should be simple yet nutritious, focusing on whole, nutrient-dense foods. Lean proteins, whole grains, fruits, and vegetables are staples, with an emphasis on options that are easy to eat and digest. Finger foods, like small sandwiches, cut-up fruits, or bite-sized vegetables, are particularly helpful for individuals who struggle with utensils or sitting through a full meal. For those with waning appetites, smaller, more frequent meals throughout the day can help maintain energy and ensure adequate nutrient intake. The familiarity of food also plays a role; meals they've enjoyed in the past often evoke positive memories and encourage eating.

Creating a peaceful mealtime environment can further support the process. Turn off televisions or other distractions, and use calm, uncluttered dining spaces to help the individual focus on their meal. The act of eating can sometimes become overwhelming or confusing, so a simple, distraction-free environment reduces stress and promotes engagement. Patience during mealtime is essential. If eating takes longer than expected, offering gentle encouragement or demonstrating by taking a bite yourself can help guide your loved one through the process.

Hydration is equally important but often overlooked in dementia care. Individuals with dementia may not recognize thirst or may forget to drink altogether, making dehydration a common risk. Caregivers can make hydration more appealing by offering drinks in visually inviting ways. Using brightly colored cups or serving beverages like fruit-infused water, herbal teas, or milkshakes can draw attention and make drinking more enjoyable. Small, frequent offerings of liquids throughout the day are often more manageable than expecting someone to drink a full glass at once. Including hydrating foods, such as watermelon, oranges, soups, and cucumbers, adds additional water content to their diet without feeling like a chore.

Adaptive utensils and dishware can play a critical role in making mealtime more manageable and less frustrating. Tools like weighted utensils or utensils with larger, easy-grip handles are useful for individuals experiencing tremors or reduced dexterity. Bowls with higher edges or plate guards can prevent spills, while non-slip placemats keep dishes stable during meals. Choosing dishware with strong contrasting colors helps make the food more visible, reducing confusion and encouraging independent eating. For example, a dark-colored plate for lighter foods can make it easier for the individual to distinguish between their meal and the plate itself.

Monitoring for nutritional deficiencies is an ongoing responsibility for caregivers. Signs of deficiencies, such as weight loss, fatigue, or behavioral changes, may indicate a need to adjust the diet or introduce supplements. Healthcare professionals and dietitians are valuable resources for evaluating and addressing specific dietary needs. Supplements, when necessary, should always be used under medical supervision to avoid any potential interactions with medications.

Mealtime is more than just providing sustenance; it is an opportunity for connection and a chance to preserve dignity. Sitting down to eat together fosters a sense of routine and inclusion. Even if communication is limited, the shared experience of a meal can create moments of connection and reassurance. Rituals such as lighting a candle or saying a few words before eating can turn mealtime into a comforting routine, offering both nourishment and emotional support.

Through careful meal planning, creative hydration strategies, adaptive tools, and attention to nutritional needs, caregivers can transform the challenges of mealtime into an opportunity for care and connection.

Personal Hygiene: Tips and Tricks for Caregivers

Personal hygiene is a fundamental aspect of caregiving that directly impacts the health, comfort, and dignity of individuals with dementia. However, these tasks often present challenges as cognitive decline affects memory, perception, and cooperation. Caregivers can navigate these difficulties by establishing routines, prioritizing dignity and privacy, using adaptive equipment, and employing gentle techniques to encourage cooperation.

Developing a consistent routine for personal hygiene is a cornerstone of effective caregiving. Predictability helps individuals with dementia feel more comfortable and reduces anxiety about what is happening. Aligning hygiene routines with the individual's prior habits and preferences can make the process smoother. For instance, if your loved one was accustomed to bathing in the evening, maintaining that timing can provide a sense of familiarity. Structuring hygiene tasks at the same time each day, such as brushing teeth after breakfast or bathing before bedtime, establishes a pattern that becomes easier to follow. Gentle reminders or visual cues, like laying out toiletries or setting up the bathroom, can also help signal that it's time for personal care.

Maintaining dignity and privacy is essential during personal care tasks. Dementia can make individuals feel vulnerable, particularly when they need assistance with intimate activities like bathing or toileting. Caregivers can preserve dignity by explaining each step of the process in a calm and reassuring tone, allowing the individual to feel informed and respected. Closing doors, using towels for coverage during bathing, or involving them in manageable aspects of the task —such as holding a washcloth—can foster a sense of autonomy. Avoid rushing through these moments, as a calm and respectful approach helps build trust and reduces resistance.

Adaptive equipment can make personal hygiene safer and more manageable for both the individual and the caregiver. Bath chairs and handheld showerheads provide stability and flexibility during bathing, while non-slip mats and grab bars in the bathroom enhance safety. Raised toilet seats or commode chairs can make toileting more accessible, reducing strain for individuals with mobility issues. Electric toothbrushes, easy-grip hairbrushes, and other grooming aids can simplify tasks that require fine motor skills. These tools not only facilitate hygiene but also support independence, enabling the person with dementia to contribute to their care as much as possible.

Resistance to hygiene tasks is a common challenge, often stemming from confusion, fear, or discomfort. Gentle techniques can help encourage cooperation while minimizing stress for both the individual and the caregiver. Offering choices, such as selecting between two outfits or deciding whether to shower before or after breakfast, gives a sense of control and involvement. Distraction can also be a powerful tool; playing soothing music, engaging in light conversation, or creating a calming environment with warm lighting can shift focus away from the task at hand. When resistance arises, it's important to remain patient and avoid confrontation. Instead, step back, reassess, and try again later when the individual may be more receptive.

Flexibility is key to overcoming resistance. Some individuals with dementia may develop sensitivities to water temperature, soap scents, or the sensation of certain grooming tools. Adapting to their preferences, such as using unscented products or adjusting water temperature, can make the process more comfortable. Additionally, breaking hygiene routines into smaller, manageable steps—such as washing one body part at a time—can reduce overwhelm.

Caregivers should also be mindful of their own emotions during hygiene routines. Frustration or impatience can inadvertently escalate resistance, so maintaining a calm and positive demeanor is essential.

Taking deep breaths, pausing when needed, and approaching each task as an opportunity to connect rather than a chore can help foster a more positive experience for both parties.

Personal hygiene is about more than cleanliness; it is a way to maintain health, preserve dignity, and nurture connection. By establishing routines, respecting privacy, utilizing adaptive equipment, and gently encouraging cooperation, caregivers can transform these often-challenging tasks into moments of care and trust.

Enhancing Communication with Your Loved One

Effective communication is a cornerstone of dementia caregiving, yet it becomes increasingly challenging as the disease progresses. Language abilities often decline, making traditional verbal exchanges difficult. However, communication extends far beyond words. Non-verbal cues such as body language, facial expressions, and tone of voice can convey care and understanding, creating a bridge between the caregiver and their loved one. By emphasizing non-verbal communication, simplifying language, practicing active listening, and using visual aids and gestures, caregivers can maintain meaningful connections and reduce frustration.

Body language and facial expressions are powerful tools in communicating with someone who has dementia. A warm smile, relaxed posture, and gentle gestures can convey reassurance and positivity even when words fail. Conversely, crossed arms, tense facial expressions, or abrupt movements can inadvertently communicate frustration or impatience, which may heighten confusion or distress in the individual. Caregivers should remain mindful of their non-verbal signals, using open and inviting gestures that align with their verbal communication. For example, leaning in slightly when speaking shows attentiveness, while maintaining eye contact reinforces connection and trust.

Tone of voice is equally significant, often carrying more weight than the words themselves. A calm, gentle, and steady tone can help soothe agitation and encourage cooperation, while a loud or sharp tone might escalate tension. Even when correcting misunderstandings or addressing behavioral challenges, a reassuring tone fosters a sense of safety and respect. Caregivers should also be aware of the pace at which they speak, slowing down to allow the individual time to process and respond.

Simplifying language is another key strategy in communicating effectively with someone with dementia. Complex sentences or abstract concepts can be overwhelming and difficult to follow. Instead, use short, clear sentences with familiar words. For instance, instead of asking, "Would you prefer to have lunch now or later after we finish errands?" try, "Would you like lunch now?" Breaking down instructions into one-step tasks also reduces confusion. While simplifying language, it's important to remain respectful and avoid sounding patronizing. Speak as you would to any adult, ensuring that your tone and phrasing reflect the dignity they deserve.

Active listening is an essential component of meaningful communication. Individuals with dementia may struggle to express themselves clearly or take longer to respond. Caregivers can show patience by maintaining eye contact, nodding to show understanding, and refraining from interrupting or finishing their sentences. It's important to give them the time and space to find their words, even if their message seems fragmented. Listening actively also involves paying attention to non-verbal cues from the individual, such as gestures, facial expressions, or changes in tone, which often reveal their emotions and needs.

Visual aids and gestures can further enhance communication, providing context and clarity when words fall short. Pictures, flashcards, or written cues can help convey messages or prompt recognition. For instance, showing a photo of food options can help your loved one choose a meal, while pointing to a clock can illustrate when it's time for an activity. Gestures, like pointing to a chair when asking someone to sit or miming brushing teeth, can provide additional context and make instructions easier to understand. These tools allow caregivers to support understanding while reducing frustration for both parties.

Combining these approaches creates a communication style that adapts to the needs and abilities of the individual with dementia. Caregivers should also remain flexible, adjusting their methods based on what works best in the moment. Some days, verbal communication may flow more easily, while on others, non-verbal cues or visual aids might be more effective. What matters most is the effort to connect and the demonstration of care and empathy through every interaction.

Communication in dementia care is not about perfect understanding but about creating moments of connection and trust. By emphasizing non-verbal communication, simplifying language, practicing patience, and incorporating visual aids, caregivers can bridge the gaps that dementia creates and foster a sense of reassurance and closeness.

Managing Sleep Issues and Sundowning

Sleep issues, including the phenomenon of sundowning, are common challenges in dementia caregiving. These disturbances can disrupt the daily lives of both the individual with dementia and their caregiver, creating frustration, exhaustion, and heightened anxiety. Understanding sundowning, developing effective evening routines, addressing environmental factors, and knowing when to seek professional consultation are key to managing these difficulties and promoting restful nights.

Sundowning refers to a pattern of increased confusion, agitation, and restlessness that often occurs in the late afternoon or evening. While the exact cause of sundowning is not fully understood, it is thought to stem from disruptions in the body's internal clock, combined with fatigue and sensory overload accumulated throughout the day. Symptoms may include pacing, wandering, repetitive questions, or irritability, all of which can interfere with winding down for the night. For caregivers, these behaviors can feel particularly challenging during a time when they, too, are likely tired and ready for rest.

Establishing a calming evening routine is one of the most effective ways to reduce sundowning symptoms and prepare for better sleep. A consistent schedule helps signal to the individual with dementia that it is time to transition from daytime activities to rest. Start with soothing, low-energy activities, such as listening to soft music, reading, or engaging in simple puzzles. Gradually move toward bedtime with predictable steps like brushing teeth, changing into pajamas, and dimming the lights. Warm baths can also be helpful for relaxation, provided they are part of the individual's preferences and do not cause distress. Avoid stimulating activities, large meals, or caffeine in the hours leading up to bedtime, as these can exacerbate agitation or delay sleep onset.

Environmental factors play a significant role in managing sleep issues and sundowning. Adjustments to the sleeping environment can create a sense of calm and security. Soft, warm lighting during the evening helps ease the transition from day to night, while blackout curtains in the bedroom can block light pollution that might disrupt sleep. Minimize noise levels, especially in the hours before bedtime, and use white noise machines or calming nature sounds to drown out unexpected disturbances. Ensure the bedroom is comfortable, with a suitable mattress, pillows, and blankets that meet the individual's preferences.

It's also important to address any safety concerns in the sleeping environment, particularly for individuals prone to wandering. Motion sensors, door alarms, or strategically placed furniture can prevent accidents while allowing caregivers to monitor movement discreetly. Having a small nightlight in the room can provide reassurance without being overly bright, helping the individual navigate their space if they wake during the night.

Despite caregivers' best efforts, some sleep issues may persist, requiring professional consultation. If sundowning symptoms or sleep disturbances are severe, frequent, or significantly impact the well-being of either the individual or their caregiver, it may be time to seek medical advice. Healthcare professionals can evaluate potential underlying causes, such as pain, medication side effects, or coexisting conditions like sleep apnea, that may be contributing to the problem.

In some cases, non-pharmacological therapies, such as light therapy or cognitive-behavioral approaches, can help regulate sleep patterns and reduce agitation. If necessary, medications like melatonin or sedatives may be considered as a short-term solution, but these should always be used under close medical supervision to avoid unwanted side effects or interactions with other treatments.

Addressing sleep issues is an integral part of dementia care, as restful nights are essential for the physical and emotional well-being of both the individual with dementia and their caregiver. However, sundowning and sleep disturbances often reflect deeper behavioral and psychological challenges, which can arise throughout the day as well as during nighttime hours.

In the next chapter, we will explore strategies for managing agitation, anxiety, depression, and other behavioral symptoms associated with dementia, equipping caregivers with tools to handle these complex situations with confidence and empathy. Let's delve into the heart of these behavioral and psychological challenges and discover ways to navigate them effectively.

FOUR

Behavioral and Psychological Challenges

Recognizing and Handling Agitation and Aggression

Agitation and aggression are among the most challenging behavioral symptoms of dementia, presenting emotional and physical risks for both the individual and the caregiver. These behaviors often arise from a combination of environmental, physical, and emotional triggers, rather than intentional hostility. Understanding the root causes of agitation and aggression, employing effective de-escalation techniques, prioritizing safety, and seeking professional support are essential for managing these episodes with empathy and effectiveness.

Identifying the triggers behind agitation and aggression is the first step in addressing these behaviors. Common triggers include pain or discomfort, hunger or thirst, overstimulation, unfamiliar environments, or an inability to communicate needs. For example, a person with dementia may become aggressive when they feel rushed during a task they don't understand, such as getting dressed. Emotional triggers like fear, frustration, or feelings of helplessness can also contribute, particularly if the individual perceives a loss of control. Caregivers can benefit from observing patterns in behavior, such as noting specific times of day or situations when agitation is more likely to occur, to preemptively address potential triggers.

When agitation or aggression occurs, employing de-escalation techniques can help diffuse the situation and restore calm. Maintaining a calm demeanor is crucial, as individuals with dementia often mirror the emotions of those around them. Speak in a soft, reassuring tone, and avoid raising your voice, which can escalate tension. Minimize external stimuli by turning off televisions, dimming lights, or moving to a quieter space. Giving the person space and avoiding direct confrontation or physical restraint can also prevent further escalation.

Validation is another effective technique for de-escalating agitation. Rather than contradicting or correcting the person's perception, acknowledge their feelings and provide reassurance. For instance, if they insist they need to "go home," instead of saying, "You are home," try responding with, "Tell me about your home. It sounds like an important place to you." This approach redirects the conversation without invalidating their experience, helping to reduce feelings of frustration or fear.

Safety is paramount during episodes of aggression. Caregivers should position themselves in a way that allows for easy exit if necessary, avoiding standing directly in front of or over the individual, which may feel threatening. Remove potentially dangerous objects from the immediate vicinity, such as sharp items or heavy furniture that could be thrown. If the situation feels unsafe, caregivers should not hesitate to step away momentarily to ensure their own safety and give the individual time to calm down.

Consistent routines and clear communication can also play a preventative role, reducing the likelihood of agitation by creating a predictable and supportive environment. For instance, maintaining a regular schedule for meals, activities, and rest helps minimize confusion and frustration. Using simple, clear instructions and offering choices—such as, "Would you like to wear the blue shirt or the green one?"—can empower the individual and reduce resistance to tasks.

When agitation and aggression persist despite these efforts, seeking professional support is critical. Healthcare professionals can evaluate underlying causes, such as untreated pain, infections, or medication side effects, that may contribute to behavioral changes. In some cases, specialists in dementia care or behavioral therapy can offer tailored strategies for managing challenging behaviors. Medication may also be considered for severe or persistent aggression, but it should be used as a last resort and under close medical supervision, given the potential for side effects.

Caregivers should also prioritize their own well-being while managing these challenges. Support groups, counseling, and respite care can provide much-needed emotional relief and practical advice from others who have navigated similar situations. Caregivers are not alone in facing these difficulties, and seeking help is a sign of strength, not failure.

Agitation and aggression can be daunting, but with patience, observation, and the right strategies, these behaviors can often be managed effectively. By addressing triggers, employing de-escalation techniques, and seeking professional guidance, caregivers can foster a safer, more supportive environment for their loved one and themselves.

Strategies for Dealing with Wandering

Wandering is a common and potentially dangerous behavior in individuals with dementia. It often stems from a variety of causes, including confusion, restlessness, or unmet needs. For caregivers, managing wandering involves implementing preventative measures, understanding its underlying causes, creating safe opportunities for movement, and preparing for emergencies. A thoughtful approach not only minimizes risks but also supports the individual's need for autonomy and exploration.

Preventative measures are the first line of defense against wandering. Making modifications to the home environment can help keep individuals with dementia safe while maintaining their freedom of movement. Door alarms, motion sensors, and pressure-sensitive mats can alert caregivers if their loved one attempts to leave the home. Installing locks on doors that are out of reach or difficult to operate provides an additional layer of security. GPS tracking devices, whether worn as a bracelet, necklace, or discreetly placed in clothing, can help caregivers locate their loved one quickly if they wander out of sight. Labeling doors with signs like "Do Not Enter" or camouflage techniques, such as painting doors to blend into walls, can also deter wandering.

Understanding the reasons behind wandering behavior is critical for addressing it effectively. Wandering is often an expression of an unmet need or a response to environmental triggers. For example, an individual may wander because they are searching for something familiar, such as their former home or workplace, or because they feel anxious or bored. Physical discomfort, such as pain or the need to use the bathroom, can also prompt wandering. Caregivers can observe patterns in behavior and look for clues that indicate the underlying cause. Addressing these root issues—whether it's ensuring regular bathroom breaks, reducing anxiety, or providing engaging activities—can reduce the likelihood of wandering episodes.

Creating opportunities for safe exploration allows individuals with dementia to satisfy their desire to move and explore without compromising safety. Designating a controlled environment, such as a secure garden, fenced yard, or enclosed indoor space, provides a sense of freedom while minimizing risks. Caregivers can create walking paths or activity stations within these areas to encourage physical activity and mental stimulation. Offering simple tasks, such as sorting objects or watering plants, can provide a sense of purpose and fulfillment, reducing the need to wander elsewhere.

Emergency preparedness is a crucial component of managing wandering. Despite preventative efforts, there is always a risk that an individual with dementia may leave the home or designated area unexpectedly. Having a detailed plan in place ensures caregivers can act quickly and effectively in such situations. Keep an up-to-date photograph of your loved one, along with a list of identifying details, such as their height, weight, and any distinguishing marks. Providing this information to local authorities can expedite search efforts if they go missing. Many communities offer programs like the Alzheimer's Association's Safe Return or Project Lifesaver, which register individuals with dementia and provide resources for locating them if they wander.

Caregivers should also inform neighbors, friends, and local businesses about their loved one's condition and provide contact information in case they are spotted wandering nearby. It's important to teach children or other family members in the household what to do in an emergency, ensuring everyone knows how to respond calmly and efficiently.

Balancing safety with dignity is essential in addressing wandering behavior. While it is important to implement preventative measures, caregivers should strive to understand wandering not as a problem to eliminate but as a behavior that reflects unmet needs or desires. By addressing these needs, providing safe spaces for exploration, and preparing for emergencies, caregivers can support their loved one's well-being while ensuring their safety.

Wandering, like many behaviors associated with dementia, requires patience, creativity, and vigilance. It is a behavior that challenges caregivers to find solutions that protect their loved one while respecting their autonomy.

Overcoming Resistance to Care

Resistance to care is a common and emotionally challenging behavior faced by dementia caregivers. It often arises from fear, confusion, or a sense of lost autonomy, and it can manifest during tasks such as bathing, dressing, or eating. An empathetic approach, combined with strategies like incremental task breakdown, involvement in decision-making, and positive reinforcement, can help reduce resistance while fostering a cooperative and trusting relationship.

An empathetic approach is the foundation for addressing resistance to care. Rather than focusing solely on completing the task at hand, caregivers should strive to understand the emotions driving the resistance. Fear is a frequent cause, especially during activities like bathing or grooming, which may feel invasive or unfamiliar. Confusion about why a task is necessary or what it entails can also lead to resistance, as can frustration over a perceived loss of control. By viewing resistance as a form of communication, caregivers can respond with patience and reassurance. Simple statements like, "I know this feels hard right now, but I'm here to help," or, "Let's take this one step at a time," validate the individual's feelings and create a sense of safety.

Breaking down care tasks into smaller, more manageable steps is a practical way to reduce overwhelm and ease resistance. For example, instead of presenting the entire process of bathing as a single task, start with one simple step, like washing hands or feet, before moving on to the next. This approach minimizes feelings of being rushed or pressured and allows the individual to adjust gradually. Giving clear, concise instructions for each step and pausing between them provides time for understanding and cooperation. For instance, instead of saying, "Let's get you ready for bed," break it into smaller requests like, "Let's brush your teeth," followed by, "Let's change into pajamas."

Involving the person with dementia in their care to the extent possible can also foster a sense of autonomy and reduce resistance. Offering choices, even small ones, empowers the individual and helps them feel more in control of the situation. For example, ask, "Would you like to wear the blue shirt or the green one?" or, "Do you want to start with your hair or your hands?" Giving them a sense of agency reinforces their dignity and encourages participation in the process. For tasks that involve personal boundaries, like bathing, asking for permission—"Can I help you with this?"—respects their autonomy and builds trust.

Positive reinforcement is another powerful tool in managing resistance to care. Recognizing and praising cooperation, no matter how small, reinforces positive behavior and fosters an encouraging atmosphere. Comments like, "You're doing a great job," or, "Thank you for letting me help," show appreciation and create a sense of accomplishment. Smiling, maintaining a warm tone, and celebrating small victories turn care tasks into opportunities for connection rather than conflict.

Caregivers should also be prepared to adapt when resistance persists. If a particular task seems too distressing in the moment, it's okay to take a step back and try again later. Recognizing when to pause and regroup helps prevent escalating tension and demonstrates sensitivity to the individual's emotional state. Using distractions or redirection can also be helpful; for instance, playing favorite music, engaging in light conversation, or incorporating a calming activity like folding towels can shift focus away from the task and reduce resistance.

Ultimately, managing resistance to care requires patience, creativity, and a deep commitment to empathy. By understanding the emotions behind resistance, breaking tasks into manageable steps, involving the individual in their care, and offering positive reinforcement, caregivers can navigate these challenges with compassion and skill. These strategies not only make care tasks more manageable but also strengthen the bond between the caregiver and their loved one, reinforcing a foundation of trust and mutual respect.

Addressing Paranoia and Hallucinations

Paranoia and hallucinations can be among the most distressing behavioral symptoms of dementia, both for the individual experiencing them and for their caregiver. These symptoms, which might manifest as false beliefs—such as accusations of theft—or as sensory experiences that aren't real, like seeing or hearing things that aren't present, require a careful and empathetic approach. While these behaviors are challenging, they can often be managed effectively through reassurance, environmental adjustments, distraction, and, when needed, medical intervention.

When an individual with dementia experiences paranoia or hallucinations, they are reacting to perceptions that feel entirely real to them, even if those perceptions don't align with reality. For example, they may accuse a family member of stealing something they misplaced or claim to see people who aren't there. The first and most important response from a caregiver is reassurance. Validating the person's feelings, rather than dismissing or contradicting their experience, helps de-escalate fear or frustration. Instead of arguing, try acknowledging their emotions. For example, if they believe someone is in the room, respond calmly with, "That must feel upsetting. Let's take a look together." This approach shows understanding and provides comfort without reinforcing the false belief.

Comforting non-verbal communication also plays a crucial role. A soft tone of voice, open body language, and gentle touch can provide reassurance. Offering a warm hand or a comforting gesture conveys support, even if words are difficult to process. Caregivers should maintain a calm demeanor, as the person with dementia is likely to pick up on and mirror the caregiver's emotional state.

Environmental factors often contribute to paranoia and hallucinations, and adjustments to the surroundings can help minimize triggers. Shadows, reflective surfaces, or even patterns on furniture or wallpaper can be misinterpreted. For example, a mirror might lead someone to believe another person is in the room, or shadows cast by furniture might appear as threatening shapes. Removing mirrors, ensuring adequate lighting, and maintaining a consistent and uncluttered environment can reduce these misinterpretations. Soft, warm lighting helps create a calming atmosphere, particularly in the evening when hallucinations or paranoia may intensify. Personalizing spaces with familiar objects like photographs or favorite keepsakes can further ground the individual and reduce feelings of confusion or fear.

Distraction is another valuable tool for managing paranoia and hallucinations. Redirecting the person's attention to a calming activity can help shift their focus away from distressing thoughts or perceptions. For example, if someone is fixated on a perceived intruder, suggesting a walk, engaging in a favorite hobby, or playing soothing music can help redirect their attention. Sensory activities, such as folding soft towels, petting a therapy animal, or enjoying a warm drink, provide comfort and create a focus on the present moment. The goal is to guide the individual toward a positive experience without directly challenging their perception.

While non-pharmacological approaches are often effective, there are times when medical intervention may be necessary. Persistent or severe paranoia and hallucinations can be exacerbated by underlying medical conditions such as infections, dehydration, or medication side effects. A healthcare professional can evaluate these factors and recommend adjustments to treatment plans. In some cases, medications may be prescribed to alleviate symptoms, but these should be approached with caution due to potential side effects and interactions. Caregivers should always consult with a physician to ensure the safest and most effective approach.

It is also essential for caregivers to take care of their own emotional health when managing these challenging behaviors. Witnessing paranoia or hallucinations in a loved one can be deeply unsettling, and caregivers may feel helpless or overwhelmed. Support groups, counseling, or simply connecting with other caregivers can provide validation and practical advice. Sharing experiences with others who understand the unique challenges of dementia caregiving helps caregivers build resilience and feel less isolated.

Addressing paranoia and hallucinations in individuals with dementia requires patience, empathy, and a willingness to adapt. These behaviors are not deliberate but are symptoms of a brain struggling to process sensory information correctly. By focusing on reassurance, modifying the environment to reduce triggers, utilizing distraction techniques, and seeking professional guidance when necessary, caregivers can create a safer and more supportive environment for their loved one. Through these strategies, the moments of fear and confusion can be mitigated, replaced instead with calm and connection.

The Role of Routine in Minimizing Behavioral Issues

A consistent daily routine serves as an anchor for individuals with dementia, offering a sense of structure and predictability that can greatly reduce behavioral challenges. As the disease progresses, cognitive decline can make each day feel unfamiliar and overwhelming. A well-established routine provides a framework that helps orient the individual, easing anxiety and creating a smoother flow to daily activities. By establishing consistency, adapting to the person's natural rhythm, incorporating enjoyable activities, and allowing for flexibility, caregivers can create a routine that supports emotional well-being and minimizes disruptive behaviors.

Consistency is key to building a routine that fosters stability and reduces confusion. When activities such as meals, bathing, and rest occur at the same time each day, the predictability reassures individuals with dementia and helps them anticipate what comes next. This structure reduces the need for decision-making and eliminates uncertainty, which are common sources of stress. For example, starting the day with a familiar morning ritual—like a favorite breakfast followed by light stretches—sets a positive tone. Over time, these patterns become ingrained, creating a comforting rhythm that guides the person through their day.

It's equally important to adapt the routine to the individual's natural pace and energy levels. People with dementia often have fluctuations in their energy and focus throughout the day, so caregivers should align activities with these natural rhythms. For instance, tasks that require concentration, such as doctor's visits or engaging in cognitive exercises, might be scheduled during the morning when energy levels are higher. Conversely, calming activities, like listening to music or taking a short walk, can be placed in the afternoon or evening when fatigue may set in. Tailoring the routine to the person's needs ensures that the schedule feels manageable and promotes cooperation.

Including activities that the person enjoys is essential for enhancing their mood and minimizing behavioral challenges. Meaningful activities—whether it's gardening, painting, or reminiscing with photo albums—provide a sense of purpose and joy. These moments of engagement can prevent boredom and restlessness, which often lead to agitation or other disruptive behaviors. Simple pleasures, like listening to a favorite song or enjoying a cup of tea in the garden, can become cherished parts of the daily routine that uplift the person and create opportunities for connection.

While consistency is vital, flexibility within the routine is equally important. Dementia care requires an adaptable approach, as each day can bring new challenges or changes in mood and ability. Some days, the individual may feel more energetic and ready to engage, while on others, they might need more rest or quieter activities. Caregivers should remain attuned to these fluctuations and adjust the routine accordingly. For instance, if a planned outing feels overwhelming, replacing it with a low-energy activity like watching a favorite movie can help maintain the flow of the day without causing distress. Flexibility allows caregivers to respond to the individual's needs while preserving the overall structure of the routine.

Routines benefit caregivers as much as they do the person with dementia. Having a clear plan for the day reduces the stress of decision-making and provides a sense of control amidst the unpredictability of caregiving. A consistent routine also creates space for caregivers to anticipate moments of respite, whether during the individual's rest periods or scheduled activities that allow for independent engagement.

The role of routine in minimizing behavioral issues underscores the importance of both structure and adaptability in dementia care. By creating a daily schedule that aligns with the individual's needs and preferences, caregivers can foster a sense of stability, reduce stress, and enhance the overall quality of life for their loved one.

As we transition into the next chapter, we'll explore strategies for caregivers to strengthen their emotional well-being, manage the stress of caregiving, and build the resilience needed to navigate the challenges of dementia care with confidence and compassion. Let's move forward into this essential discussion of self-care and emotional support.

FIVE

Building Resilience and Emotional Strength

The Importance of Self-Care for Caregivers

Caregiving for someone with dementia is a profound act of love and dedication, but it is also physically and emotionally demanding. Amid the daily challenges, caregivers often neglect their own needs, prioritizing their loved one's well-being above all else. While this selflessness is admirable, it can lead to burnout, exhaustion, and a diminished capacity to provide effective care. Embracing self-care as an essential component of caregiving allows caregivers to maintain their health, resilience, and emotional strength, enabling them to support their loved ones more effectively.

Prioritizing self-care is not a selfish act; it is a necessity. When caregivers neglect their own health and emotional needs, they risk burnout, which can manifest as fatigue, irritability, depression, or physical illness. These challenges not only affect the caregiver's well-being but can also compromise the quality of care they provide. By viewing self-care as an integral part of caregiving, rather than an indulgence, caregivers can reframe their priorities to include their own health and happiness. A caregiver who takes time to recharge is better equipped to navigate the complexities of dementia care with patience, compassion, and clarity.

Simple, actionable strategies can make self-care an attainable goal, even in the busiest caregiving schedules. Physical activity is a cornerstone of self-care, as it promotes both physical health and mental well-being. Even short walks, yoga sessions, or light stretching exercises can reduce stress, boost energy levels, and improve mood. Healthy eating is equally important; caregivers often skip meals or rely on convenient, less nutritious options due to time constraints. Preparing simple, balanced meals and staying hydrated can significantly improve overall health and resilience. Adequate rest is another non-negotiable aspect of self-care. Sleep disruptions are common among caregivers, especially those caring for individuals with dementia who experience sundowning or nighttime wandering. Prioritizing rest, whether by seeking respite care, sharing responsibilities with others, or taking short naps, helps combat the exhaustion that caregiving can bring.

Setting boundaries is essential for preventing caregiver burnout and protecting personal well-being. Many caregivers feel obligated to be available at all times, which can lead to feelings of being overwhelmed or resentful. Learning to say no, delegating tasks, or asking for help when needed are acts of strength, not weakness. Setting clear boundaries also involves carving out dedicated time for oneself, whether it's a weekly exercise class, a quiet hour for reading, or time to connect with friends. Communicating these boundaries to family members, friends, or professional caregivers helps ensure that the caregiver's needs are respected and prioritized alongside those of their loved one.

Seeking personal joy is an often-overlooked aspect of self-care, but it is vital for maintaining emotional health. Pursuing activities or hobbies that bring fulfillment outside of the caregiving role can create a sense of balance and renewal. Whether it's gardening, painting, listening to music, or simply enjoying a favorite TV show, these moments of joy remind caregivers of their individuality and provide a break from the demands of caregiving. Engaging in these activities without guilt is crucial; caregivers must recognize that taking time for themselves ultimately benefits both them and their loved ones.

Self-care for caregivers is not about escaping responsibilities but about sustaining the strength needed to meet them. By prioritizing their own well-being, caregivers create a foundation for resilience, enabling them to face challenges with greater patience and emotional stability.

Techniques for Managing Caregiver Stress

Stress is an inevitable part of caregiving, particularly when supporting a loved one with dementia. The physical, emotional, and logistical demands can accumulate, leading to feelings of overwhelm and burnout if left unchecked. Managing caregiver stress is not only essential for personal well-being but also for maintaining the capacity to provide effective care. By recognizing signs of stress, practicing stress reduction techniques, improving time management, and seeking professional help when needed, caregivers can build resilience and approach their role with greater balance and confidence.

Recognizing the signs of stress is the first step in addressing it. Many caregivers become so focused on their responsibilities that they fail to notice the toll stress takes on their health and emotional state. Common signs include fatigue, irritability, difficulty concentrating, frequent headaches, and changes in appetite or sleep patterns. Emotional symptoms, such as feelings of helplessness, anger, or persistent sadness, may also emerge. Early recognition of these signs allows caregivers to take proactive steps before stress becomes overwhelming. Acknowledging these feelings without judgment is crucial; stress does not mean a lack of capability or love—it's a natural response to the challenges of caregiving.

Stress reduction techniques are valuable tools for regaining balance. Practices like meditation and mindfulness help caregivers stay grounded and manage emotional reactivity. Even just a few minutes of focused breathing can lower stress levels and create a sense of calm. Deep breathing exercises, where one inhales deeply through the nose, holds the breath for a count, and exhales slowly through the mouth, can be done anywhere and are particularly effective during high-stress moments. Mindfulness, which involves staying present and accepting the moment without judgment, encourages caregivers to let go of worries about the past or future, reducing anxiety and promoting clarity.

Physical activity is another powerful stress reliever. Exercise releases endorphins, the body's natural stress fighters, and helps improve sleep and overall energy levels. Whether it's a brisk walk, a yoga class, or a few stretches during the day, regular movement offers both physical and mental health benefits. Journaling can also serve as an outlet for processing emotions and reflecting on the caregiving journey. Writing down thoughts and feelings provides a sense of release and helps caregivers identify patterns or triggers contributing to their stress.

Effective time management is a practical way to alleviate the pressure of caregiving. Creating a schedule that prioritizes essential tasks while leaving room for rest and flexibility can prevent caregivers from feeling overwhelmed by competing demands. Tools like to-do lists, calendars, and reminders help organize responsibilities and reduce the mental load of remembering everything. Delegating tasks to other family members, friends, or professional caregivers is also essential for managing time and conserving energy. Recognizing that it's okay to ask for help is a critical aspect of time management; caregivers do not need to shoulder every responsibility alone.

Professional help is a vital resource for managing caregiver stress. Therapy or counseling provides a safe space for caregivers to explore their feelings, develop coping strategies, and gain perspective on their role. Mental health professionals can offer tools tailored to the caregiver's unique challenges, helping them navigate the emotional complexities of caregiving. Support groups, whether in person or online, provide connection and validation from others who share similar experiences. These groups foster a sense of community and offer practical advice, reducing the isolation that caregivers often feel.

Respite care is another form of professional support that allows caregivers to take regular breaks while ensuring their loved one receives quality care. Whether for a few hours, a day, or a weekend, respite care provides an opportunity to rest, recharge, and return to caregiving with renewed energy. Caregiving is a demanding role, and seeking external support is a sign of strength, not weakness.

Managing caregiver stress is about creating balance, building resilience, and embracing the resources available to support your well-being. By recognizing stress early, practicing relaxation techniques, managing time effectively, and seeking professional help, caregivers can navigate the challenges of dementia care with greater ease and emotional stability. These strategies not only enhance the caregiver's quality of life but also enable them to provide better care for their loved ones.

Finding and Utilizing Support Networks

Caregiving for someone with dementia can feel isolating, but it doesn't have to be a solitary journey. Support networks are invaluable for caregivers, offering both emotional and practical benefits that ease the challenges of caregiving. By finding support groups, building a personal network, and leveraging social media, caregivers can connect with others who understand their experiences, share advice, and offer encouragement.

Support networks provide caregivers with a sense of community and understanding. Being part of a group where others share similar challenges and triumphs can validate feelings and alleviate the loneliness that often accompanies caregiving. These connections create a safe space to share frustrations, celebrate successes, and seek advice without fear of judgment. On a practical level, support networks offer resources, insights, and tips that can simplify caregiving tasks. For example, members may share strategies for managing difficult behaviors, navigating medical systems, or accessing financial assistance. The collective knowledge of a support network often provides solutions that caregivers might not discover on their own.

Finding support groups tailored to dementia caregivers is an excellent starting point. Local community centers, hospitals, and nonprofit organizations often host in-person support groups that foster connections among caregivers in the same geographic area. These meetings provide a chance to share experiences face-to-face, build relationships, and learn from guest speakers or facilitators with expertise in dementia care. For those unable to attend in-person meetings, online support groups offer flexibility and accessibility. Websites like the Alzheimer's Association or caregiver-focused forums often host virtual groups, allowing caregivers to connect with others across the globe from the comfort of their homes. Social media platforms like Facebook also feature groups dedicated to dementia caregiving, where members can post questions, share advice, and offer support around the clock.

Building a personal support network is equally important. Friends, family members, neighbors, and community resources can form the backbone of a caregiver's support system. Start by reaching out to those who are willing and able to help. Clear communication about what you need—whether it's help with errands, companionship for your loved one, or simply someone to talk to—makes it easier for others to offer meaningful assistance. Don't hesitate to ask for specific help, such as, "Could you sit with Mom for a couple of hours while I run errands?" or, "Would you mind cooking a meal for us once a week?" When people know exactly how they can help, they're more likely to step in.

Community resources, such as senior centers, faith-based organizations, and local nonprofits, often provide additional support. These services might include respite care, caregiver training, or access to legal and financial planning. Reaching out to these organizations not only expands your support network but also helps you access resources designed to lighten the caregiving load.

Social media is another powerful tool for connecting with other caregivers. Platforms like Facebook, Twitter, and Instagram host vibrant caregiving communities where individuals share their experiences, celebrate victories, and provide support during tough times. Joining groups or following accounts dedicated to dementia caregiving can help you find valuable advice, tips, and a sense of camaraderie. Many caregivers use social media to share their own stories, raising awareness about the realities of dementia care and finding solidarity with others who understand their journey. However, it's important to maintain privacy and be selective about the information shared online. Ensure that any personal or medical details are shared only in trusted and secure groups.

Support networks offer far-reaching benefits, from reducing stress and isolation to providing practical solutions and fostering emotional resilience. Caregiving is an intense and demanding role, but with the support of a strong network, it becomes more manageable and less isolating.

Nurturing Your Own Mental and Emotional Health

The mental and emotional health of caregivers is just as important as the physical well-being of the person they are caring for. Caregiving for someone with dementia brings unique challenges, requiring caregivers to be not only physically present but emotionally available, often for long periods. The emotional toll of this role can be profound, ranging from feelings of sadness and frustration to moments of joy and connection. By understanding emotional needs, adopting effective coping mechanisms, maintaining emotional balance, and seeking professional support when necessary, caregivers can nurture their own mental health and continue to provide compassionate care.

Understanding and acknowledging your own emotional needs is the first step toward fostering emotional well-being. Caregivers often focus so intensely on their loved one's needs that they neglect their own emotions, dismissing them as unimportant or secondary. However, unaddressed feelings of grief, anger, guilt, or anxiety can accumulate, leading to burnout or depression. Caregivers should take time to reflect on their emotions and recognize that these feelings are valid and natural responses to the challenges of caregiving. Journaling, talking with a trusted friend, or simply sitting quietly to process emotions can help caregivers stay in touch with their inner experiences.

Coping mechanisms play a vital role in managing the emotional toll of caregiving. Engaging in mindfulness practices, such as meditation or yoga, can provide moments of calm and clarity amidst the chaos. Deep breathing exercises, which involve slow, deliberate inhalations and exhalations, are particularly useful during stressful moments, helping to reduce tension and regain focus. Physical activity, whether it's a walk in the park, a dance class, or gardening, also serves as a powerful outlet for releasing stress and boosting mood. Creative pursuits, such as painting, knitting, or playing music, offer an opportunity to express emotions in a constructive and fulfilling way.

Maintaining emotional balance amidst the ups and downs of caregiving requires intentional effort. One of the most effective strategies is setting realistic expectations for yourself. Caregivers often feel pressured to meet impossible standards, leading to feelings of failure or inadequacy when those expectations aren't met. Acknowledging that caregiving is inherently imperfect and focusing on the effort rather than the outcome can alleviate self-imposed guilt.

Another key strategy is creating boundaries that protect your emotional energy. Caregiving is a demanding role, and it's easy to feel consumed by its responsibilities. Setting aside dedicated time for yourself—whether for rest, hobbies, or social interactions—helps maintain balance and prevents burnout. Open communication with family members and friends about your emotional needs can also foster understanding and support, allowing others to step in when you need a break.

Seeking joy in small moments can also help caregivers maintain a positive outlook. Whether it's enjoying a cup of coffee, laughing over a shared memory, or simply appreciating a quiet moment, finding gratitude in everyday experiences builds emotional resilience. While caregiving comes with its share of challenges, focusing on the love and connection that underpin the role can be a source of comfort and strength.

Professional mental health support is a critical resource for caregivers who find themselves struggling to cope. Therapy or counseling provides a safe space to explore feelings, develop coping strategies, and address underlying concerns. Mental health professionals can offer tools tailored to the unique challenges of caregiving, helping individuals navigate emotions like grief, anger, or guilt. Support groups also offer emotional validation and practical advice from others who understand the complexities of dementia caregiving. These connections can reduce feelings of isolation and foster a sense of community.

Caregivers should not hesitate to seek help if they notice signs of emotional distress, such as persistent sadness, irritability, or difficulty concentrating. Addressing mental health concerns early prevents them from escalating and supports overall well-being. Self-compassion is essential; caregivers must remind themselves that seeking help is not a sign of weakness but an act of strength and self-preservation.

Nurturing mental and emotional health is not a luxury for caregivers—it is a necessity. By acknowledging their emotions, adopting effective coping strategies, maintaining balance, and seeking professional support when needed, caregivers can build the resilience required to navigate the caregiving journey. This self-care ultimately benefits not only the caregiver but also their loved one, ensuring that care is given with patience, compassion, and emotional clarity.

Overcoming Isolation in the Caregiving Journey

Caregiving for a loved one with dementia can often feel like a lonely path. The demands of caregiving, combined with the emotional weight of watching a loved one decline, can lead to feelings of isolation that affect a caregiver's physical and mental health. Recognizing and addressing these feelings is critical to maintaining balance and finding fulfillment in the caregiving journey. By identifying isolation, implementing strategies to combat it, and leveraging the tools of connection—including technology—caregivers can rediscover a sense of community and support.

Identifying isolation begins with acknowledging its presence and understanding its impact. Many caregivers become so immersed in their responsibilities that they neglect their social lives, distancing themselves from friends, family, and activities they once enjoyed. Signs of isolation may include feelings of loneliness, irritability, or sadness, as well as a lack of energy or interest in reaching out to others. This isolation can lead to burnout, depression, and a sense of disconnection that makes caregiving feel even more overwhelming.

Recognizing these patterns is the first step in addressing them and finding ways to reconnect.

Practical strategies for combating isolation focus on re-establishing a sense of community. Joining caregiver support groups, whether in person or online, allows caregivers to connect with others who understand their challenges. These groups provide a safe space to share experiences, seek advice, and simply feel heard. Community activities, such as attending local events or participating in hobbies, offer opportunities to interact with others and step away from caregiving for a while. Volunteering, even in small ways, can be a meaningful way to reconnect with a broader sense of purpose and meet new people.

Maintaining connections with friends and family is another vital strategy for reducing isolation. Caregivers often hesitate to reach out, either because they feel their friends or family won't understand or because they're reluctant to burden others with their struggles. However, loved ones can be an invaluable source of support if caregivers are open about their needs. Inviting friends over for a casual visit, having regular phone calls, or even meeting for a short walk can rekindle connections. Sharing caregiving updates and experiences also helps friends and family understand the caregiver's world, fostering empathy and stronger relationships.

Technology offers powerful tools for staying connected and overcoming physical barriers to social interaction. Video calls through platforms like Zoom or FaceTime enable caregivers to maintain meaningful relationships, even when they cannot leave their homes. Social networking sites and online forums provide a space to share stories, seek advice, and build relationships with caregivers from around the world. These platforms can also serve as a source of inspiration, offering practical caregiving tips and emotional encouragement. Caregivers should explore these tools to find the platforms that best suit their needs and comfort levels.

Combating isolation not only benefits caregivers emotionally but also enhances their ability to care for their loved one. A caregiver who feels connected, supported, and understood is more likely to approach their role with patience and compassion. These renewed connections can also serve as a reminder that caregiving is not a solitary journey—there is a network of individuals, both near and far, who can provide guidance, companionship, and encouragement.

As caregivers take steps to rebuild their connections with the world, they can also focus on strengthening their bond with their loved one. Caregiving is not just about meeting physical needs; it is also about nurturing a relationship that continues to evolve despite the challenges of dementia.

In the next chapter, we will explore ways to foster emotional closeness, engage meaningfully, and celebrate moments of joy with your loved one, reinforcing the deep connection that caregiving can sustain. Let's continue the journey together.

SIX

Connecting with Your Loved One

Communicating Through the Barriers of Dementia

Communication is one of the most profound ways to connect with a loved one, but dementia introduces barriers that can make this fundamental act challenging. As cognitive changes affect memory, language, and comprehension, caregivers must adapt their communication styles to maintain connection and understanding. By embracing empathy, using non-verbal cues, and ensuring that interactions preserve dignity, caregivers can foster meaningful connections despite the barriers of dementia.

Adapting communication styles is essential as dementia progresses. Simple strategies, such as speaking more slowly, using short sentences, and focusing on one idea at a time, can make it easier for your loved one to follow conversations. Avoid complex or abstract language, instead opting for clear and direct phrases. For example, instead of saying, "Let's get ready for dinner and then we'll watch TV," try, "It's time to eat now." Using the individual's name to gain their attention before speaking and maintaining eye contact helps establish focus. These adjustments ensure that communication feels manageable rather than overwhelming.

Listening with empathy is another cornerstone of effective communication. Dementia often alters how individuals perceive and interpret their surroundings, leading to moments of confusion or inaccurate statements. Instead of correcting them, which can increase frustration or shame, focus on validating their feelings. If your loved one insists on going to a job they retired from years ago, respond with, "That job was so important to you. Tell me more about it," rather than pointing out the inaccuracy. This approach shifts the focus from factual correctness to emotional connection, reducing stress and fostering a sense of understanding.

Non-verbal communication becomes increasingly important as verbal abilities decline. A smile, gentle touch, or warm tone of voice can convey love and reassurance when words are hard to find. Body language speaks volumes; leaning in slightly when your loved one is speaking shows attentiveness, while maintaining a calm and open posture communicates that you are present and engaged. Visual cues, such as pointing to objects or demonstrating actions, can help clarify your words and provide context. For example, holding up a sweater while asking, "Would you like to wear this?" combines verbal and non-verbal communication for better comprehension.

Maintaining dignity in communication is essential to preserving your loved one's sense of self-worth. Even as dementia changes how they interact with the world, they remain an individual with preferences, feelings, and a lifetime of experiences. Avoid speaking about them as if they are not present or talking down to them in a patronizing tone. Instead, include them in conversations and decisions whenever possible, asking for their input in a way that feels respectful. Small acts, like waiting patiently for them to respond or rephrasing a question if they struggle, reinforce their value and capability.

Finding joy in communication involves shifting expectations. While dementia may limit traditional conversations, meaningful exchanges can still occur in the present moment. Singing a favorite song together, sharing a smile, or reminiscing over a photograph can create shared experiences that transcend words. Even silence can be powerful when paired with a reassuring touch or shared presence.

Communication is not just about transferring information—it is about connection, understanding, and love. Adapting your approach, listening with empathy, using non-verbal cues, and prioritizing dignity transforms these moments into opportunities to strengthen your bond with your loved one.

Utilizing Music and Art for Emotional Expression

Music and art possess unique abilities to transcend the barriers created by dementia, offering caregivers and their loved ones powerful tools for connection, emotional expression, and joy. These creative outlets allow individuals with dementia to communicate and engage in meaningful ways, even when verbal communication becomes difficult. Through music, art therapy, shared creative projects, and the documentation of life stories, caregivers can foster emotional connections that deepen their bond with their loved one.

Music has an extraordinary capacity to connect individuals with their emotions and memories. Familiar songs, in particular, can evoke strong emotional responses, tapping into parts of the brain that remain intact even as dementia progresses. Playing a favorite tune from their youth or a cherished family anthem can spark recognition, elicit smiles, and even encourage movement, such as clapping or gentle dancing. Singing together provides a shared experience that strengthens emotional ties. For caregivers, observing the joy and connection music brings to their loved one offers moments of fulfillment and affirmation.

Music can also serve as a therapeutic tool for calming agitation or uplifting mood. Gentle, soothing melodies are effective for creating a relaxing atmosphere during stressful moments, while more upbeat rhythms can invigorate and energize. Incorporating music into daily routines—such as playing a morning playlist during breakfast or a calming song before bedtime—provides structure and enhances the caregiving experience. Caregivers should consider creating personalized playlists tailored to their loved one's preferences, ensuring that the music resonates deeply and positively.

Art therapy provides another avenue for self-expression and communication. Dementia often limits the ability to articulate thoughts and emotions verbally, but art offers a non-verbal outlet for creativity and storytelling. Painting, drawing, or working with clay allows individuals to explore their feelings and engage with their environment in a tactile, meaningful way. Caregivers can encourage participation by providing simple tools, such as washable paints, crayons, or modeling clay, and celebrating the process rather than focusing on the outcome.

Art therapy is not limited to the person with dementia; caregivers, too, can benefit from engaging in artistic activities as a way to process their emotions and find solace. Creating side-by-side offers opportunities for mutual engagement and reinforces the bond between caregiver and loved one. Whether it's painting together or sharing in the joy of crafting a simple collage, these moments foster connection while allowing both parties to express themselves.

Shared creative projects strengthen bonds and create a sense of accomplishment. Collaborating on a quilt, scrapbook, or photo album provides a tangible representation of the memories and moments shared. Projects like decorating a small garden pot, making holiday ornaments, or creating greeting cards offer opportunities for laughter, teamwork, and pride in a joint effort. The process of working together is as important as the finished product, providing opportunities for conversation, reminiscing, and joy.

Music and art also offer meaningful ways to document life stories and preserve memories. Listening to songs that were significant during certain periods of life can prompt storytelling and reflection. A familiar tune might lead to a memory of a first dance, a family gathering, or a favorite vacation. Caregivers can capture these moments by writing down anecdotes or creating a playlist that reflects the soundtrack of their loved one's life.

Art, too, can serve as a medium for documenting memories. A scrapbook filled with drawings, photos, or notes offers a visual record of experiences and emotions. Engaging in these activities together ensures that the caregiver and their loved one share in preserving the individual's unique legacy.

Utilizing music and art as tools for emotional expression enriches the caregiving journey, creating moments of connection and joy that endure beyond words. These creative avenues honor the personhood of individuals with dementia, providing opportunities for self-expression, engagement, and mutual connection.

The Power of Touch and Physical Connection

Physical touch is one of the most fundamental forms of communication, capable of conveying love, reassurance, and comfort without the need for words. For individuals with dementia, who may struggle with verbal communication or experience feelings of isolation, touch can bridge the gap and create a deep sense of connection. By employing comforting touch techniques, respecting personal boundaries, and offering non-intrusive physical comfort, caregivers can use this simple yet profound tool to strengthen their bond with their loved one.

The importance of physical touch in caregiving cannot be overstated. Human touch has been shown to release oxytocin, a hormone that promotes feelings of trust and reduces stress, benefiting both the giver and receiver. For individuals with dementia, who often feel disconnected or misunderstood, a gentle touch can communicate care and presence more effectively than words. Holding hands during a walk, placing a reassuring hand on their shoulder, or offering a warm embrace provides a sense of security and reminds them they are not alone. Physical touch, especially when paired with eye contact and a calm voice, helps establish a sense of grounding and emotional stability.

Comforting touch techniques can be simple yet impactful. Hand massages, for instance, are a soothing way to engage physically and emotionally. Using a light lotion or oil, caregivers can gently rub the palms, fingers, and backs of the hands, creating a calming sensory experience that fosters relaxation. Hugs can provide immediate comfort and warmth, while a gentle pat on the back or stroking of the arm can convey reassurance. Brushing or combing hair is another tactile activity that can be both comforting and reminiscent of familiar care rituals. These techniques help reduce anxiety, soothe agitation, and enhance the overall caregiving experience.

Respecting personal boundaries is critical when using physical touch to connect with someone who has dementia. While touch is powerful, it must always be offered with consideration for the individual's preferences and comfort level. Dementia can alter how physical sensations are perceived, and some individuals may find certain types of touch unsettling or invasive. Observing cues, such as flinching, pulling away, or verbal objections, helps caregivers determine what types of touch are acceptable. Always ask for permission before initiating physical contact, even in subtle ways, such as saying, "May I hold your hand?" This approach ensures that touch is received as a gesture of care rather than an unwelcome intrusion.

Non-intrusive ways to offer physical comfort can be just as effective as direct touch. For individuals who may be resistant to physical contact, caregivers can use strategies that promote comfort while maintaining personal space. Offering a soft blanket to hold, placing a pillow or cushion in their lap, or encouraging them to cuddle with a pet or stuffed animal provides tactile reassurance without crossing boundaries. Sitting close by and mirroring their body language can also create a sense of presence and connection without requiring direct contact.

Touch is particularly meaningful during moments of distress or confusion. A hand placed gently on the back or a supportive arm around the shoulders can help calm agitation and convey empathy. These simple gestures provide a tangible reminder of love and support, reducing feelings of fear or uncertainty. When paired with other comforting techniques, such as a soothing tone of voice or calming music, touch can become an integral part of emotional care.

For caregivers, using touch to connect with a loved one also offers its own rewards. The act of providing physical comfort fosters a sense of closeness and reaffirms the caregiver's role in providing reassurance and stability. These moments of connection serve as powerful reminders of the bond that persists despite the challenges of dementia.

The power of touch lies in its ability to communicate beyond words, offering solace and strengthening the caregiver-loved one relationship. By being attuned to preferences, employing gentle techniques, and respecting boundaries, caregivers can use physical connection to nurture a sense of love and trust, enriching the caregiving journey.

Creating Meaningful Activities Together

Shared activities are a powerful way to connect with a loved one who has dementia, offering moments of joy, engagement, and emotional closeness. Meaningful activities provide both the caregiver and the person with dementia opportunities to create positive experiences and deepen their bond. By carefully selecting activities, adapting them to abilities, and fostering new traditions, caregivers can use these shared moments to enrich their relationship and provide comfort amidst the challenges of dementia.

Choosing activities that are meaningful and enjoyable for both the caregiver and the person with dementia starts with considering their past interests, preferences, and abilities. Activities should resonate with the individual's personality and evoke positive memories. For example, a former gardener might enjoy planting flowers or tending to indoor plants, while someone who loved cooking might take pleasure in simple kitchen tasks like stirring batter or arranging ingredients. Caregivers should also choose activities they enjoy, creating shared moments that feel natural and fulfilling for both parties. The key is to focus on the experience rather than the outcome, allowing the activity to unfold without pressure or expectations.

Adapting activities to the person's current abilities ensures that participation feels empowering rather than frustrating. Dementia often brings changes in fine motor skills, memory, and concentration, so activities should be tailored to match the individual's capabilities. For instance, if they enjoy art but find painting challenging, caregivers might offer crayons or pre-drawn coloring sheets as a simpler alternative. Games with fewer rules, puzzles with larger pieces, or crafts that involve tactile elements like gluing or tearing paper can provide similar enjoyment with less complexity. Breaking tasks into smaller steps and providing gentle guidance allows the individual to engage comfortably without feeling overwhelmed.

Creating new traditions and routines that incorporate meaningful activities adds structure and anticipation to the day. Simple rituals, such as an afternoon tea with favorite treats, a weekly movie night, or a morning walk, create moments to look forward to and foster a sense of continuity. These traditions don't need to be elaborate; even small, repeated activities carry emotional weight and build shared experiences. Seasonal traditions, like decorating for holidays, baking cookies, or crafting ornaments, can become cherished rituals that provide a sense of normalcy and joy.

The role of activities in relationship building cannot be overstated. Shared experiences help caregivers and their loved ones connect on an emotional level, reinforcing the bond that may feel strained by the challenges of dementia. Activities provide a context for communication, whether through reminiscing about old times while looking through photo albums or laughing together over a lighthearted game. These moments of connection remind both caregiver and loved one of their shared history and the relationship that endures despite the changes dementia brings.

Activities also serve as a way to shift focus from caregiving tasks to moments of pure enjoyment. They create opportunities for laughter, conversation, and mutual appreciation, transforming the dynamic from caregiver and care recipient to two people sharing time together. This shift fosters a sense of partnership and equality, which can be particularly meaningful for individuals who feel the loss of independence brought on by dementia.

Caregivers should also remain flexible and open to experimenting with different activities. Preferences and abilities may change over time, and what works one day might not resonate the next. Staying attuned to the individual's mood and responses helps caregivers adjust their approach, ensuring that the activity remains engaging and enjoyable. Even quiet, unstructured moments, like sitting together to watch birds or listen to music, can be profoundly meaningful.

Creating meaningful activities together is about finding ways to connect, celebrate, and enjoy the present moment. By choosing activities thoughtfully, adapting them to current abilities, and embracing the opportunity for relationship building, caregivers can create shared experiences that bring comfort and joy to both their loved one and themselves.

Celebrating Small Victories and Joyful Moments

In the journey of caregiving, the path is often fraught with challenges and emotional highs and lows. Amid these difficulties, finding and celebrating small victories and joyful moments provides a much-needed balance, offering a source of positivity and hope. These celebrations, however modest, serve as reminders of the love and connection that persist despite the changes brought by dementia. By recognizing progress, documenting moments of joy, maintaining a positive outlook, and sharing successes, caregivers can foster a more uplifting caregiving experience for themselves and their loved ones.

Recognizing and celebrating progress, no matter how small, is a vital practice for caregivers. Success doesn't always mean significant milestones; it can be as simple as a smile, a moment of engagement, or a task completed with less assistance. These moments, though fleeting, hold immense value. A loved one remembering a familiar face, enjoying a shared laugh, or participating in an activity that once seemed out of reach are all victories worth celebrating. Acknowledging these achievements reinforces the caregiver's efforts and provides motivation to continue fostering positive interactions.

Documenting joyful moments creates a tangible record of these shared experiences, preserving them for reflection and encouragement. Caregivers can keep a journal to jot down heartwarming anecdotes, meaningful conversations, or small milestones. Photographs or videos of these moments can also serve as visual reminders of the joy that caregiving brings. These records not only uplift caregivers during difficult times but also provide a way to honor the journey they've undertaken with their loved one. Revisiting these memories reinforces the enduring connection and love that caregiving nurtures.

The power of positivity cannot be overstated in the caregiving journey. Maintaining an optimistic outlook helps caregivers approach their role with resilience and compassion. Positivity doesn't mean ignoring challenges or suppressing difficult emotions—it's about finding light in the moments that make the journey worthwhile. A positive attitude can also have a profound effect on the person with dementia, creating an environment of warmth and encouragement. Caregivers who exude patience and optimism often find that their loved one mirrors those emotions, fostering an atmosphere of mutual care and understanding.

Sharing successes and joyful moments with others is another way to amplify positivity and create a sense of community. Whether it's recounting a funny anecdote to friends, posting a photo in an online caregiver group, or sharing a memory with family members, these moments connect caregivers to a broader support system. Celebrating wins together strengthens bonds within the caregiver's network and provides hope to others who may be navigating similar challenges. Hearing about another caregiver's joyful experience can inspire and remind others of the value found in caregiving.

Celebrating small victories also shifts the focus from what is lost to what is still present and meaningful. It encourages caregivers to appreciate the beauty of the present moment, even as they prepare for the uncertainties ahead. This balanced perspective helps sustain emotional health and resilience, making the caregiving journey more fulfilling and less daunting.

As the caregiving journey evolves, so too do the challenges and responsibilities. Beyond emotional connection and daily care, caregivers must navigate critical legal and financial considerations to ensure their loved one's well-being and security.

In the next chapter we will explore the essential steps caregivers need to take to protect their loved one's interests, from creating wills and powers of attorney to understanding medical directives and long-term care planning. Let's move forward into this vital area of caregiving preparation.

SEVEN

Legal Planning and Documentation

Understanding and Setting Up Power of Attorney

Planning for the legal and financial aspects of dementia care is an essential part of caregiving, and establishing a Power of Attorney (POA) is one of the most critical steps. POA is a legal document that authorizes a trusted individual—referred to as an agent or attorney-in-fact—to make decisions on behalf of someone who may become unable to do so. It provides peace of mind by ensuring that the person with dementia will have their affairs managed by someone who prioritizes their best interests. Understanding the concept of POA, the types available, the process of establishment, and addressing common misconceptions can help caregivers take this crucial step with confidence.

At its core, Power of Attorney is about protection and preparation. It enables a designated individual to act on behalf of the person with dementia in financial or healthcare matters, depending on the type of POA established. Setting up POA early in the dementia journey is vital, as the person granting the authority must have the cognitive capacity to understand and agree to the arrangement. Establishing POA proactively avoids complications or legal battles later, ensuring that decisions can be made smoothly and in alignment with the individual's wishes.

There are two primary types of POA: financial and healthcare, each serving distinct but equally important purposes. A financial POA authorizes the agent to manage financial matters, such as paying bills, managing investments, filing taxes, and handling property transactions. This ensures that financial responsibilities are maintained, even if the individual with dementia can no longer manage them independently.

Healthcare POA, on the other hand, gives the agent the authority to make medical decisions on behalf of the individual. This includes decisions about treatments, medications, surgeries, and, in some cases, end-of-life care. Healthcare POA works in tandem with advance directives, which outline the individual's medical preferences, to ensure that their wishes are honored. Both types of POA are essential for comprehensive planning, as they address different facets of care and decision-making.

The process of establishing POA involves several steps. First, the individual with dementia must choose an agent they trust implicitly. This person should be someone who understands their values and is willing and able to act in their best interests. It's important to have an open and honest discussion with the chosen agent about the responsibilities involved and to ensure they are comfortable with the role.

Once an agent is selected, the next step is to work with an attorney or legal service to draft the necessary documents. Each state or country may have specific requirements, so consulting with a legal professional ensures the POA is properly executed. In some cases, a durable POA may be established, which remains in effect even if the individual loses decision-making capacity. The document must typically be signed, notarized, and, in some jurisdictions, witnessed to be legally binding.

It's also helpful to discuss and document specific scenarios or preferences within the POA to provide the agent with clear guidance. For example, the financial POA might include instructions about managing investments, while the healthcare POA could outline preferences for palliative care or resuscitation efforts.

There are common misconceptions about POA that can cause hesitation or confusion. One frequent misunderstanding is the belief that granting POA means giving up independence. In reality, POA is a safeguard—it only comes into effect when the individual is unable to make decisions themselves. Until that point, the person retains full control over their affairs. Another misconception is that POA automatically covers all aspects of decision-making. In truth, financial and healthcare POAs must be established separately, and their scopes are defined within the legal documents.

By setting up Power of Attorney early, families can ensure that the individual with dementia is protected and their wishes are respected. This legal tool offers reassurance that someone trustworthy will handle important decisions, providing stability and security for both the individual and their caregivers.

The Essentials of Guardianship and Conservatorship

As dementia progresses, there may come a time when an individual can no longer make decisions about their personal, financial, or medical affairs, and other legal arrangements, such as Power of Attorney (POA), are not in place. In such cases, guardianship and conservatorship may become necessary. These legal tools provide a court-appointed individual with the authority to act in the best interest of the person with dementia. Understanding the distinctions between guardianship and conservatorship, the legal process, the rights and responsibilities involved, and the ethical considerations is crucial for families navigating this path.

Guardianship and conservatorship are legal mechanisms that serve different but related purposes. Guardianship typically grants authority over personal and healthcare decisions for an individual deemed incapacitated by the court. This might include decisions about living arrangements, medical treatments, and personal care. Conservatorship, on the other hand, is focused on managing an individual's financial affairs, such as paying bills, managing investments, and safeguarding assets. In some cases, a single person may serve as both guardian and conservator, but these roles can also be assigned separately, depending on the needs of the individual and the qualifications of those appointed.

The legal process for obtaining guardianship or conservatorship can be complex and varies by jurisdiction. It begins with filing a petition in court, typically by a family member or close associate, requesting the authority to act on behalf of the person with dementia. The court requires evidence that the individual is no longer capable of making informed decisions due to their cognitive condition. This evidence often includes medical evaluations, statements from healthcare providers, and sometimes testimony from caregivers or family members.

A court hearing is usually held to evaluate the petition. During this process, the person with dementia may have legal representation or a court-appointed advocate to ensure their rights are protected. The court assesses the suitability of the proposed guardian or conservator, considering their relationship with the individual, financial expertise, and ability to act in their best interest. Legal counsel is highly recommended for families navigating this process, as guardianship and conservatorship involve significant legal responsibilities and oversight.

Once appointed, guardians and conservators have defined rights and responsibilities. A guardian's duties may include making healthcare decisions, determining living arrangements, and ensuring that the individual's daily needs are met. Conservators are tasked with managing financial affairs, which includes budgeting, filing taxes, and protecting assets from misuse or fraud. Both roles require regular reporting to the court to ensure transparency and accountability. Guardians and conservators must act solely in the best interest of the person with dementia, avoiding conflicts of interest or actions that could compromise their well-being.

Ethical considerations are an integral part of deciding whether to pursue guardianship or conservatorship. These arrangements involve a significant loss of autonomy for the individual with dementia, which can be emotionally challenging for families. Before proceeding, it's important to explore all alternatives, such as mediation or supported decision-making, which allow the individual to retain as much independence as possible while receiving necessary support. Families should also reflect on their motivations, ensuring that the decision is guided by the individual's needs rather than external pressures or personal gain.

The emotional impact on families can be profound. The process often brings feelings of guilt, sadness, or conflict among family members, particularly if there is disagreement about the need for guardianship or who should take on the role. Open communication, counseling, or mediation can help families navigate these emotions and maintain unity during this challenging time.

Guardianship and conservatorship are critical tools for protecting individuals with dementia when other legal arrangements are unavailable or inadequate. By understanding the roles, navigating the legal process thoughtfully, and prioritizing ethical considerations, families can ensure that these mechanisms are used responsibly and compassionately.

Navigating Advance Directives and Living Wills

Advance directives and living wills are critical tools for safeguarding the healthcare preferences of individuals with dementia, ensuring that their wishes are respected even if they can no longer communicate or make decisions for themselves. These documents provide clarity and guidance to caregivers and healthcare providers, reducing uncertainty and potential conflicts during challenging times. Understanding their importance, components, creation process, and legal considerations equips families with the knowledge to take proactive steps in care planning.

Advance directives are legal documents that outline an individual's preferences for medical care and appoint a trusted person to make healthcare decisions on their behalf if they are unable to do so. For individuals with dementia, establishing advance directives early in the disease progression is essential, as it requires cognitive capacity to articulate and formalize these preferences. Having these directives in place provides peace of mind, ensuring that care aligns with their values and wishes, while alleviating the burden on family members who might otherwise have to make difficult decisions without clear guidance.

The two primary components of advance directives are living wills and healthcare proxy designations. A living will specifies the individual's preferences for medical treatments, particularly in situations involving life-sustaining interventions. For instance, it may address decisions about artificial nutrition and hydration, ventilator use, or resuscitation efforts. A healthcare proxy designation, often referred to as a durable medical Power of Attorney (POA), appoints a trusted individual to act as the decision-maker for medical care when the person with dementia is no longer able to make choices independently. These components work together to ensure both specific preferences and unforeseen medical situations are addressed.

Creating a living will involves thoughtful discussions and clear documentation. Caregivers should encourage their loved ones to have open conversations with family members and healthcare providers about their values and priorities regarding medical care. These discussions might explore questions like, "What does quality of life mean to you?" or, "Are there certain treatments you would or would not want in a critical situation?" Such conversations provide a foundation for drafting a living will that accurately reflects the individual's wishes.

Once preferences are clear, the next step is to formalize them in writing. Working with an attorney or using reputable advance directive forms tailored to the individual's state ensures the document complies with legal requirements. Witness signatures or notarization may be needed for the document to be legally valid, depending on local laws. Caregivers should also encourage their loved one to appoint a healthcare proxy who is not only trustworthy but also capable of handling potentially complex or emotional medical decisions. The chosen proxy should understand the individual's preferences thoroughly and feel confident advocating for them when necessary.

Legal validity and accessibility of advance directives are paramount to their effectiveness. A legally valid advance directive ensures that healthcare providers and institutions honor the specified wishes. Caregivers should confirm that the document adheres to state-specific regulations and consider reviewing it periodically to ensure it remains up to date and relevant.

Equally important is making the advance directive easily accessible to all relevant parties. Copies should be shared with family members, the appointed healthcare proxy, and primary care providers. It's also helpful to have a copy included in the individual's medical records at hospitals or other healthcare facilities. Some caregivers choose to store a copy in a prominent location in the home, such as a folder marked "Medical Documents," for quick access during emergencies.

Advance directives and living wills offer families the reassurance that their loved one's healthcare preferences will be honored, even in the face of difficult circumstances. By addressing these decisions early, caregivers and their loved ones create a foundation of clarity, trust, and respect, reducing stress and conflict during critical moments.

Legal and Ethical Considerations in Dementia Care

Caregiving for someone with dementia involves navigating a complex landscape of legal and ethical challenges. From balancing autonomy and safety to making decisions about end-of-life care, caregivers often face dilemmas that test their judgment and compassion. Understanding the ethical principles at play, as well as the legal rights of individuals with dementia, equips caregivers to approach these situations with sensitivity and confidence. By addressing ethical dilemmas, respecting legal rights, navigating informed consent, and approaching end-of-life decisions thoughtfully, caregivers can provide care that honors the dignity and individuality of their loved one.

Ethical dilemmas are an inevitable part of dementia care, particularly when a person's cognitive abilities decline but their desire for independence remains strong. For example, caregivers might grapple with whether to restrict certain activities, such as driving or managing finances, to ensure safety while respecting their loved one's autonomy. Decisions about moving to a care facility, implementing safety measures in the home, or managing aggressive behaviors also raise ethical questions. In these situations, caregivers should aim to strike a balance between protecting their loved one and honoring their preferences. Engaging the individual in discussions, whenever possible, and seeking input from healthcare providers or ethics committees can help caregivers navigate these challenges with greater clarity.

The legal rights of individuals with dementia remain intact throughout the disease progression, even as decision-making capacity diminishes. These rights include the right to dignity, the right to make decisions when capable, and the right to privacy and informed consent. Caregivers must ensure that decisions about care, living arrangements, and medical treatment are made in a manner that respects these rights. When making decisions on behalf of their loved one, caregivers should prioritize what the individual would have wanted based on past conversations, values, and cultural or religious beliefs.

Informed consent becomes increasingly complex as dementia advances. Informed consent requires that the individual understands the risks, benefits, and alternatives of a proposed treatment or action. However, as cognitive abilities decline, the ability to comprehend and weigh decisions diminishes. In early stages, individuals may still have the capacity to make decisions about their care, and caregivers should facilitate open discussions with healthcare providers to ensure the person understands their options. As decision-making capacity fades, the responsibility often shifts to a legally appointed decision-maker, such as a healthcare proxy or guardian. Caregivers in this role must base decisions on the individual's documented preferences, values, or previously expressed wishes, ensuring that their choices align with the person's best interests.

End-of-life decisions are among the most sensitive and emotionally charged aspects of dementia care. These decisions often involve topics such as do-not-resuscitate (DNR) orders, palliative care options, and the use of life-sustaining treatments. Caregivers should address these matters early in the dementia journey, while the individual is still capable of articulating their preferences. Discussing advance directives and including specific instructions about end-of-life care helps ensure that the person's wishes are honored when they can no longer communicate them.

Palliative care, which focuses on comfort and quality of life rather than curative treatments, is an important option to consider as dementia progresses. Families may also face decisions about withholding or withdrawing life-sustaining interventions, such as feeding tubes or ventilators. These decisions require caregivers to weigh the benefits and burdens of treatment, often consulting with healthcare providers, hospice teams, or spiritual advisors for guidance. The goal is to ensure that care aligns with the individual's values and provides dignity and comfort in their final stages of life.

Legal and ethical considerations in dementia care require careful thought and a commitment to honoring the rights and humanity of the individual. By addressing dilemmas compassionately, respecting legal rights, navigating informed consent appropriately, and making thoughtful end-of-life decisions, caregivers can provide care that is both ethically and legally sound.

Protecting Assets and Planning for Long-Term Care

As dementia progresses, the financial demands of caregiving can become overwhelming. From home care and assisted living to skilled nursing facilities, the costs of long-term care can deplete savings if not planned for carefully. Protecting assets and planning for these expenses is crucial for ensuring financial security while accessing the care your loved one needs. By employing asset protection strategies, understanding long-term care insurance, navigating Medicaid planning, and incorporating estate planning, caregivers can create a comprehensive financial strategy that honors their loved one's wishes and safeguards their legacy.

Asset protection strategies are essential for preserving financial resources while maintaining eligibility for government assistance programs like Medicaid. One approach involves transferring assets to trusted family members or placing them in irrevocable trusts, which can protect them from being counted toward Medicaid eligibility. However, it is important to be mindful of Medicaid's look-back period—a window of time, usually five years, during which any significant asset transfers may result in penalties or delays in eligibility. Families should consult with an elder law attorney to navigate these complexities and avoid unintended consequences.

Gifting strategies can also help preserve assets while providing for loved ones. For example, gifting small amounts within the limits of tax exemptions can reduce the overall estate value without triggering tax liabilities. Properly structuring these gifts ensures they are given in compliance with regulations and aligned with long-term financial goals. Similarly, joint ownership or designating payable-on-death beneficiaries for certain accounts can simplify the process of transferring assets and reduce probate costs.

Long-term care insurance plays a critical role in offsetting the costs of care. This type of insurance is designed to cover expenses related to home care, assisted living, memory care, and skilled nursing facilities. Families considering long-term care insurance should evaluate policies carefully, paying attention to factors such as the daily benefit amount, the length of coverage, and inflation protection. Policies with flexible terms that cover a range of care settings offer the greatest utility as needs evolve. It's worth noting that premiums tend to be more affordable when purchased earlier in life, so families should explore this option as part of proactive planning.

Medicaid planning is an integral component of financial preparation for dementia care, especially when personal funds or long-term care insurance are insufficient to cover expenses. Medicaid is a joint federal and state program that provides assistance for low-income individuals, including coverage for long-term care services. Eligibility requirements vary by state, but generally, individuals must meet strict income and asset thresholds. Spend-down strategies—where individuals reduce their countable assets to meet Medicaid limits—are often necessary. This might include paying off debts, prepaying funeral expenses, or making necessary home modifications. Working with a Medicaid planning expert ensures that these strategies are executed effectively and in compliance with regulations.

Estate planning is another crucial element in protecting assets and ensuring that the person with dementia's wishes are fulfilled. Creating or updating a will is foundational, as it specifies how assets should be distributed upon their passing. Trusts, such as irrevocable or special needs trusts, can offer additional protection and flexibility. For example, a special needs trust allows families to set aside funds for the benefit of the person with dementia without affecting their eligibility for government assistance programs.

Advance planning tools, like transfer-on-death deeds or beneficiary designations, simplify the transfer of assets and reduce the burden on surviving family members. Caregivers should also consider appointing an executor or trustee who will carry out the estate plan in accordance with the person's wishes.

Protecting assets and planning for long-term care requires foresight, professional guidance, and a commitment to honoring the needs and preferences of the person with dementia. These strategies not only safeguard financial security but also provide peace of mind for both caregivers and their loved ones.

In this next chapter, we'll explore practical strategies for budgeting, identifying funding resources, and leveraging financial assistance programs to support the ongoing costs of caregiving.

EIGHT

Financial Strategies and Assistance

Budgeting for Dementia Care Costs

Managing the financial challenges of dementia care is a critical aspect of the caregiving journey. From medical expenses to day-to-day living costs, the financial demands can quickly become overwhelming without a clear plan. Creating a budget tailored to dementia care ensures that resources are allocated efficiently, reducing stress and allowing caregivers to focus on providing quality care. By identifying costs, developing a care budget, implementing cost-saving strategies, and seeking professional guidance, caregivers can navigate the financial complexities with confidence.

Identifying the various costs associated with dementia care is the first step in creating a realistic budget. Care expenses can vary significantly depending on the stage of dementia, the level of care required, and the available resources. Typical costs include medical expenses such as doctor visits, medications, and therapy sessions. Additionally, caregivers must consider the cost of personal care items like incontinence products, adaptive clothing, and mobility aids. For those relying on professional caregiving support, costs may include in-home care services, adult day programs, or fees for assisted living or skilled nursing facilities. Beyond these direct care expenses, indirect costs, such as transportation, home modifications, or respite care, should also be factored into the budget.

Once all potential expenses are identified, creating a comprehensive care budget provides a framework for managing these costs. Start by listing all income sources, such as pensions, Social Security benefits, or retirement accounts, alongside the identified expenses. Categorize these costs into fixed (e.g., rent, insurance premiums) and variable (e.g., groceries, utilities) to gain a clearer picture of financial needs. Technology tools, such as budgeting apps or spreadsheets, can simplify this process and make it easier to track expenses over time. Including an emergency fund within the budget is also essential, as dementia care often involves unexpected costs, such as hospitalizations or the need for additional caregiving support.

Cost-saving strategies can help caregivers manage expenses without compromising the quality of care. For example, buying in bulk or using subscription services for recurring items like incontinence products can reduce costs. Caregivers may also qualify for discounts or assistance programs offered by pharmaceutical companies or nonprofits for medications and medical equipment. Exploring local resources, such as food banks or community transportation services, can further alleviate financial strain. Another effective strategy is to prioritize spending on high-impact items and services, focusing on what will most directly enhance the well-being of the person with dementia.

Negotiating rates with service providers or facilities is another potential avenue for cost savings. Some in-home care agencies or assisted living facilities may offer sliding-scale fees or discounts for longer-term commitments. Caregivers should also investigate tax credits or deductions available to those providing care for a loved one, such as the Child and Dependent Care Credit or deductions for medical expenses.

Finally, accessing financial planning resources and professional guidance ensures a well-rounded approach to dementia care budgeting. Financial advisors specializing in elder care can provide valuable insights into managing assets, exploring long-term care insurance options, and planning for Medicaid eligibility. Nonprofit organizations like the Alzheimer's Association offer free resources, including budgeting templates, workshops, and access to local support groups that can share cost-saving tips. Caregivers should also consider consulting with an elder law attorney to ensure legal and financial plans are aligned, particularly when addressing asset protection or Medicaid planning.

Budgeting for dementia care requires foresight, organization, and a willingness to seek out resources and support. By identifying costs, creating a clear financial plan, implementing cost-saving strategies, and leveraging professional advice, caregivers can navigate this aspect of caregiving with greater ease and assurance. This proactive approach not only ensures that resources are used effectively but also provides caregivers with the peace of mind to focus on their loved one's needs.

Exploring Insurance Options and Benefits

Insurance can play a significant role in offsetting the costs of dementia care, but understanding the intricacies of available options is essential for making the most of these resources. From Medicare and private insurance to long-term care policies, caregivers must navigate a complex system to determine what coverage is available and how to maximize benefits. By understanding Medicare's scope, exploring private insurance options, employing strategies for benefit maximization, and learning to navigate insurance claims, caregivers can create a more comprehensive financial plan for dementia care.

Medicare is often a primary source of healthcare coverage for individuals with dementia, but its limitations must be understood. Medicare Part A covers hospital stays, skilled nursing care for a limited time, and some home health services, but it does not cover custodial care, such as assistance with bathing, dressing, or long-term care in nursing homes. Part B provides coverage for outpatient services, including doctor visits and certain therapies, while Part D offers prescription drug coverage. Medicare Advantage plans (Part C) may include additional benefits, such as transportation and caregiver support, but these vary widely by plan. Understanding these gaps is critical, as caregivers will need to plan for out-of-pocket costs or explore supplemental insurance to cover expenses Medicare does not address.

Private insurance options can complement Medicare or provide additional coverage for dementia care. Health insurance policies may include benefits for therapies, medications, or limited home health services. Disability insurance, if secured before the onset of dementia, can provide income replacement for individuals who are unable to work due to their condition. Long-term care insurance is specifically designed to cover the costs of services like in-home care, assisted living, or nursing homes. Families considering long-term care insurance should review policies carefully to understand the scope of coverage, benefit triggers, and exclusions. Policies purchased before a dementia diagnosis are more likely to provide comprehensive benefits, as most require a health assessment before approval.

Maximizing insurance benefits requires a proactive and informed approach. Start by reviewing existing policies to understand their terms, coverage limits, and exclusions. Many policies include benefits that caregivers may not immediately realize, such as coverage for respite care or adult day programs. Caregivers should contact insurance providers directly to clarify benefits and ensure they are fully utilized. For Medicare, this might involve consulting with a Medicare specialist or using free resources like the State Health

Insurance Assistance Program (SHIP) to navigate options and supplemental plans.

Navigating insurance claims can be one of the most challenging aspects of utilizing insurance for dementia care. Proper documentation is key to a successful claim. This includes maintaining accurate records of medical visits, treatments, and expenses, as well as obtaining detailed notes from healthcare providers about the necessity of services or equipment. Submitting claims promptly and following up with the insurance provider ensures that the process moves forward without unnecessary delays. If a claim is denied, caregivers should not hesitate to appeal the decision. Many initial denials are overturned during the appeals process, especially when additional supporting documentation is provided. Advocacy is often required to secure the benefits individuals are entitled to, so caregivers should be prepared to persist in their efforts.

Caregivers can also explore support services offered by insurance companies, such as case managers or care coordinators who specialize in navigating benefits for complex conditions like dementia. These professionals can provide guidance on claims, recommend covered services, and help families optimize their insurance plans.

Understanding and leveraging insurance options is an integral part of managing the financial aspects of dementia care. By clarifying Medicare coverage, exploring private insurance options, maximizing benefits, and learning to navigate claims effectively, caregivers can alleviate financial burdens and focus on providing quality care for their loved ones.

Government Aid and Assistance Programs

Government aid programs are invaluable resources for caregivers and individuals with dementia, offering financial assistance and services that can ease the financial burden of care. These programs address a range of needs, from healthcare coverage to daily living support, and provide crucial relief for families navigating the complexities of dementia care. Understanding the available programs, their eligibility criteria, the application process, and how to overcome common challenges ensures that caregivers can access the help they need.

A variety of government programs provide financial assistance or services to individuals with dementia and their caregivers. Medicaid is among the most comprehensive, covering long-term care services such as nursing home care, in-home health care, and community-based services for eligible low-income individuals. Medicaid waivers, available in many states, offer additional support for care provided in non-institutional settings, allowing individuals to remain at home or in community environments. Veterans and their families can access benefits through the Department of Veterans Affairs (VA), including Aid and Attendance, which provides financial support for veterans who need assistance with daily activities. Supplemental Security Income (SSI), a federal program for low-income individuals, can help cover basic living expenses. Additionally, state-specific programs may offer grants, respite care, or transportation assistance tailored to the needs of dementia patients and their families.

Eligibility criteria for these programs vary, and understanding them is key to determining which resources are accessible. Medicaid eligibility typically depends on income and asset thresholds, which differ by state. For example, applicants must often demonstrate limited financial resources and meet functional criteria indicating the need for long-term care services. VA benefits require proof of military service and other conditions, such as a demonstrated need for assistance with daily living. SSI eligibility focuses on income and disability status. State programs may have unique requirements, such as residency or enrollment in specific caregiving initiatives. Consulting with program representatives or elder law attorneys can help caregivers navigate these requirements and identify the most suitable options.

The application process for government aid programs can be complex, but preparation and persistence make a significant difference. Applications generally require detailed documentation, including proof of income, assets, medical diagnoses, and care needs. For Medicaid, families may need to provide bank statements, tax returns, and records of medical expenses. VA benefits require military service records, medical evidence, and documentation of caregiving needs. SSI applications involve submitting medical and financial information, along with any additional evidence supporting disability status.

Caregivers should start the application process early, as approvals can take several months. Engaging with local Area Agencies on Aging (AAAs), Medicaid offices, or VA service officers provides guidance on required documentation and helps streamline the process. Keeping organized records and copies of all submitted materials ensures that caregivers have everything needed for follow-ups or appeals.

Despite the benefits, applying for government aid programs often presents challenges. Long wait times, complex eligibility rules, and extensive paperwork can frustrate caregivers. Additionally, denials due to incomplete applications or misunderstandings of program requirements are common. To address these issues, caregivers should seek professional assistance from elder law attorneys, Medicaid planning experts, or VA-accredited representatives. These professionals can clarify requirements, ensure applications are complete, and assist with appeals if necessary. Support groups and community organizations can also provide practical advice and encouragement.

Persistence is key when navigating government programs. If an application is denied, caregivers should request detailed explanations and pursue the appeals process with additional evidence. Many denials are reversed on appeal, especially when caregivers demonstrate eligibility through thorough documentation.

Accessing government aid programs requires effort, but the support they provide is invaluable for alleviating the financial strain of dementia care. By understanding available programs, meeting eligibility criteria, preparing for the application process, and addressing challenges with determination, caregivers can unlock essential resources to support their loved ones.

Financial Aid for Home Care and Assisted Living

Home care and assisted living are two essential options for individuals with dementia, offering varying levels of support based on care needs and preferences. However, the costs associated with these services can quickly become a financial strain for many families. Understanding funding options, planning for expenses, accessing financial assistance programs, and selecting the right care providers ensures that caregivers can balance quality care with financial sustainability.

Funding options for home care services include private pay, insurance, and government programs. Private pay is the most straightforward method, where families use personal savings, income, or investments to cover the cost of care. While this approach offers flexibility, it can deplete resources quickly without proper budgeting. Long-term care insurance can help offset home care costs, covering services like personal care aides or home modifications. However, policies must be purchased before dementia diagnosis to be effective. Government programs such as Medicaid offer significant support for eligible individuals, covering home health aides, medical equipment, and community-based services. Medicaid waivers, available in many states, allow for additional home care services tailored to keeping individuals in their residences.

Assisted living costs vary widely depending on location, services, and the level of care required. On average, assisted living facilities charge monthly fees ranging from $4,000 to $6,000, but costs can climb higher for memory care units designed for individuals with dementia. Planning for these expenses involves assessing current financial resources, exploring insurance benefits, and considering government programs like Medicaid, which may cover certain aspects of assisted living. Veterans and their spouses may qualify for VA benefits, such as Aid and Attendance, which provide additional funds for assisted living costs.

Financial assistance programs are designed to bridge the gap for families struggling to afford home care or assisted living. Medicaid remains a primary source of aid, but state-specific programs and grants also offer support. For example, some states provide financial aid for adult day programs or respite care, reducing the overall cost of caregiving. Charitable organizations, such as the Alzheimer's Foundation of America, offer grants for caregiving expenses, while nonprofit groups and religious organizations may provide subsidized home care or assisted living services. Families should also explore tax deductions related to caregiving, such as medical expense deductions or dependent care credits, to alleviate some of the financial burden.

Evaluating and choosing care providers is a critical step in ensuring that quality care is delivered within the caregiver's budget. For home care services, caregivers should seek providers with experience in dementia care and verify credentials through references or reviews. Interviews with potential aides or agencies can provide insight into their approach and compatibility with the individual's needs. It's essential to confirm that the provider is licensed, insured, and compliant with state regulations.

When selecting an assisted living facility, caregivers should prioritize transparency about costs and services. Touring the facility and asking detailed questions about staff qualifications, resident-to-staff ratios, and the availability of memory care services help ensure that the chosen facility meets the individual's requirements. Observing the environment during a visit—such as cleanliness, atmosphere, and interactions between staff and residents—provides additional context. Understanding what services are included in the base fee and what incurs additional charges helps prevent financial surprises.

Families should also ask facilities or agencies about sliding scale fees or payment plans, which can make quality care more accessible. Comparison shopping and negotiating terms can further help caregivers stay within budget without sacrificing quality. If financial challenges persist, consulting with an elder care planner or financial advisor can help identify alternative solutions or maximize available resources.

Securing financial aid for home care and assisted living requires a proactive approach, combining careful planning, resource exploration, and informed decision-making. By leveraging funding options, accessing assistance programs, and thoroughly evaluating care providers, caregivers can ensure that their loved ones receive the support they need while preserving financial stability.

Managing the Cost of Medication and Treatment

The cost of dementia medications and treatments can be a significant financial burden for caregivers and families, particularly as the condition progresses and medical needs become more complex. Understanding the typical costs of medications, accessing prescription assistance programs, weighing the benefits of generic versus brand-name drugs, and implementing effective medication management strategies can help caregivers navigate these expenses while ensuring that their loved one receives necessary care.

Dementia medications often fall into two primary categories: those aimed at managing cognitive symptoms, such as cholinesterase inhibitors (e.g., donepezil, rivastigmine) and NMDA receptor antagonists (e.g., memantine), and those used to address behavioral symptoms, like antipsychotics or antidepressants. The monthly cost of these medications can range from $30 for generic options to several hundred dollars for brand-name drugs, depending on insurance coverage and local pricing. Other treatments, such as therapy or specialized medical interventions, further contribute to the financial load. Without adequate planning, these recurring expenses can quickly strain a family's resources.

Prescription assistance programs provide critical relief for families facing high medication costs. Many pharmaceutical companies offer patient assistance programs that provide free or discounted medications to those who qualify based on income or insurance status. Nonprofit organizations and government agencies, such as the Partnership for Prescription Assistance or Medicare's Extra Help program, also offer subsidies and discounts for medications. Caregivers should explore these options and apply proactively, as they can substantially reduce out-of-pocket expenses.

Choosing between generic and brand-name medications is another important consideration for managing costs. Generic drugs are typically much less expensive than their brand-name counterparts and are required by regulatory agencies to meet the same safety and efficacy standards. For many dementia-related medications, generic alternatives provide a cost-effective solution without compromising treatment outcomes. However, caregivers should consult with healthcare providers to ensure that switching to a generic option is appropriate, as individual responses to medications can vary.

Medication management strategies are essential for minimizing costs and ensuring effective treatment. Caregivers can start by working closely with healthcare providers to regularly review all prescribed medications. This review helps eliminate unnecessary or redundant medications and ensures that dosages are optimized. Exploring 90-

day prescription options through pharmacies or mail-order services can also reduce costs compared to monthly refills. Additionally, caregivers should inquire about pharmaceutical coupons or discount cards, which are often available for commonly prescribed drugs.

Organizing medications efficiently can prevent waste and ensure adherence, reducing the likelihood of missed doses or the need for additional interventions. Tools like pill organizers, automatic dispensers, or medication tracking apps can simplify the process and minimize errors. For caregivers managing multiple prescriptions, consolidating medication purchases at a single pharmacy can simplify billing and allow pharmacists to provide cost-saving recommendations.

Budgeting for medication and treatment costs should also include a contingency plan for unforeseen medical needs. While routine expenses can often be predicted, sudden changes in health may require new medications or treatments. Setting aside funds specifically for medical expenses provides flexibility and helps alleviate the stress of unanticipated costs.

Managing the cost of dementia medications and treatments requires diligence, planning, and the use of available resources. By exploring assistance programs, considering generic options, implementing cost-saving strategies, and maintaining open communication with healthcare providers, caregivers can balance financial constraints with the need to provide effective care.

As the financial aspects of caregiving are addressed, it becomes increasingly important to prepare for the broader challenges that lie ahead. In the next chapter we will explore ways to navigate end-of-life wishes, long-term care decisions, and the emotional transitions that come with advanced dementia. Let's move forward into this vital chapter of preparation and planning.

NINE

Preparing for the Future

Discussing End-of-Life Wishes

Discussing end-of-life wishes is one of the most sensitive yet necessary aspects of preparing for the future. For individuals with dementia and their caregivers, these conversations ensure that care aligns with the individual's values, reduces uncertainty for family members, and provides a clear plan for healthcare providers to follow. By approaching the topic respectfully, documenting preferences, involving healthcare providers, and fostering family alignment, caregivers can create a framework that honors their loved one's wishes while navigating this challenging journey.

Initiating a conversation about end-of-life wishes requires empathy, timing, and a safe space for open dialogue. It's important to approach the topic gently, choosing a time when the individual is calm and receptive. Framing the conversation as a way to ensure their preferences are respected can help ease anxiety. For instance, a caregiver might say, "I want to make sure that any decisions we make are what you would want. Can we talk about how you'd like things to be handled in the future?" Avoid rushing or pressuring the individual; instead, allow the discussion to unfold naturally over time. For some families, this may involve multiple conversations to address different aspects of care.

Documenting these preferences formally is essential to ensure they are understood and followed. Living wills and advanced directives are legal tools that capture an individual's wishes regarding medical interventions, such as resuscitation, feeding tubes, or palliative care. These documents also outline broader healthcare preferences, ensuring that decisions align with their values even when they can no longer communicate their choices. Caregivers should encourage their loved ones to consult with an elder law attorney or healthcare provider to create these documents, ensuring they comply with legal requirements. Copies should be shared with family members, caregivers, and healthcare providers to ensure accessibility when needed.

Healthcare providers play a vital role in these discussions, offering medical insight into what is feasible and practical in end-of-life care. Physicians and specialists can help clarify the implications of certain decisions, such as the benefits and burdens of life-sustaining treatments. Encouraging the individual to have these conversations directly with their doctor ensures that their preferences are informed by accurate medical knowledge. Caregivers can also request that these discussions be documented in the person's medical records, creating a clear directive for healthcare teams to follow in critical situations.

Involving family members in these discussions is crucial to achieving alignment and reducing the risk of future conflicts. Caregivers should consider organizing a family meeting to share and discuss the individual's wishes, ensuring that everyone understands and respects their decisions. Having a clear, documented plan helps prevent disagreements among family members and provides a united front when decisions need to be made. For families with differing views, a neutral mediator, such as a counselor or elder law attorney, can facilitate these conversations and ensure that the focus remains on honoring the individual's preferences.

Caregivers should also be prepared for emotional responses from their loved ones and family members. Discussions about end-of-life care often evoke feelings of fear, sadness, or denial. Acknowledging and validating these emotions while gently steering the conversation back to practicalities helps maintain a constructive tone. Reassuring everyone that these plans are about ensuring dignity and comfort can help alleviate some of the emotional weight of the topic.

By approaching end-of-life discussions with compassion, documenting preferences clearly, involving healthcare providers, and fostering family alignment, caregivers ensure that their loved one's values are honored. These conversations are not easy, but they provide a foundation of clarity and respect that benefits everyone involved.

Choosing the Right Long-Term Care Facility

Choosing the right long-term care facility for a loved one with dementia is a deeply personal and consequential decision. It involves finding a place that not only meets their medical and emotional needs but also offers a safe, supportive environment where they can thrive. By carefully assessing needs, evaluating facilities, planning visits effectively, and providing support during the transition, caregivers can make a decision that feels right for both their loved one and their family.

The first step is assessing the specific needs of your loved one to ensure the facility can accommodate them. This involves understanding their medical requirements, such as the level of memory care, assistance with daily activities, and management of any chronic conditions. Behavioral needs, such as handling agitation or wandering, should also be considered. Emotional and social factors, including opportunities for meaningful engagement, companionship, and personal hobbies, are equally important. Compiling a detailed list of priorities—such as proximity to family, cultural or religious considerations, and budget constraints—provides a clear framework for evaluating options.

When evaluating long-term care facilities, caregivers should prioritize a range of criteria to ensure their loved one's needs will be met. Staff qualifications and training are critical; caregivers should confirm that staff members are experienced in dementia care and have ongoing opportunities for professional development. The quality and variety of care services offered—such as memory care programs, on-site medical support, and assistance with personal care—are another key factor. The facility's environment also plays a significant role in overall well-being. A warm, clean, and welcoming atmosphere with accessible layouts, secure outdoor spaces, and appropriate safety features promotes comfort and reduces stress for residents with dementia.

Visiting potential facilities is an essential part of the decision-making process, as it provides an opportunity to observe day-to-day operations and ask questions directly. During visits, caregivers should pay attention to how staff interact with residents, noting whether they demonstrate patience, kindness, and attentiveness. Observing activities, meal times, and common areas helps gauge the facility's culture and the level of engagement it offers. Key questions to ask include:

- What is the staff-to-resident ratio, particularly for memory care units?
- How are behavioral challenges like wandering or aggression managed?
- Are there specific programs designed for residents with dementia?

- What safety measures are in place, such as secure entrances and monitoring systems?
- How does the facility communicate with families about their loved one's care?

Transitioning a loved one into a long-term care facility can be emotionally challenging for everyone involved. Supporting your loved one during this time requires patience, understanding, and preparation. Begin by involving them in the process to the extent possible, allowing them to express preferences or visit facilities before the move. Gradual transitions, such as short visits or day stays at the facility, can help familiarize them with the environment and reduce anxiety.

On moving day, caregivers should focus on creating a sense of continuity and comfort. Bringing personal belongings, like favorite photographs, blankets, or decorations, helps make the new space feel familiar. Reassuring your loved one that this move is to provide additional support while maintaining regular visits and communication strengthens their sense of security.

After the transition, staying involved in their care is essential. Regular visits, participation in care planning meetings, and maintaining open communication with staff ensure that your loved one's needs are met and any concerns are addressed promptly. Building relationships with caregivers at the facility fosters collaboration and trust, creating a supportive network for both your loved one and yourself.

Choosing the right long-term care facility requires careful planning, thorough evaluation, and emotional sensitivity. By assessing needs, visiting and evaluating facilities, and supporting your loved one during the transition, caregivers can ensure that this step in the caregiving journey provides safety, dignity, and opportunities for connection.

Palliative Care Options and Considerations

Palliative care is a specialized approach to medical care that prioritizes comfort, quality of life, and holistic support for individuals facing serious illnesses, including dementia. For caregivers and families navigating the advanced stages of dementia, understanding palliative care and when to consider it can provide a path toward compassionate and person-centered care. By exploring what palliative care involves, determining eligibility, understanding its benefits for dementia patients, and finding qualified providers, caregivers can ensure that their loved one receives care that aligns with their needs and values.

Palliative care focuses on managing symptoms, alleviating discomfort, and addressing emotional, psychological, and spiritual needs rather than seeking to cure or reverse the underlying condition. This approach differs from traditional medical care, which often prioritizes interventions and treatments aimed at prolonging life. Palliative care teams work collaboratively with patients, families, and other healthcare providers to develop individualized care plans that honor the patient's preferences and enhance their quality of life. In dementia care, this often involves managing pain, addressing behavioral symptoms, and providing emotional support to both the individual and their caregivers.

Eligibility for palliative care is based on the individual's needs rather than a specific diagnosis or prognosis. Individuals with dementia may benefit from palliative care at any stage of the disease, but it is particularly valuable in the later stages when symptoms become more complex. Caregivers should consider palliative care if their loved one experiences frequent hospitalizations, significant pain or discomfort, difficulties with eating or drinking, or profound behavioral changes. Consulting with a primary care physician or specialist can help determine if palliative care is an appropriate addition to the overall care plan.

The benefits of palliative care for individuals with dementia are profound, focusing on comfort and quality of life. Symptom management is a primary goal, with palliative care teams addressing issues such as pain, agitation, shortness of breath, and insomnia. Behavioral symptoms, such as anxiety or restlessness, are also managed with non-pharmacological approaches and, when necessary, carefully considered medications. This attention to symptom relief enhances the individual's overall well-being and reduces distress for caregivers. Palliative care also provides emotional and psychological support, helping individuals with dementia navigate feelings of fear, confusion, or frustration while offering counseling and resources to caregivers coping with the demands of caregiving.

Holistic support is a hallmark of palliative care, addressing not only physical needs but also emotional, social, and spiritual concerns. Caregivers often find solace in the guidance and reassurance provided by palliative care teams, who work to support the entire family unit. This comprehensive approach ensures that all aspects of the caregiving journey are considered and addressed with sensitivity and expertise.

Finding and choosing palliative care providers with experience in dementia care is essential to ensuring the best outcomes for your loved one. Start by seeking recommendations from your primary care physician, neurologist, or other trusted healthcare providers. Many hospitals and healthcare systems have dedicated palliative care departments, while community-based palliative care services can provide support at home or in residential settings. Online directories, such as those offered by the National Hospice and Palliative Care Organization (NHPCO) or the Alzheimer's Association, can help caregivers identify local providers. When evaluating providers, caregivers should ask about their experience with dementia care, the services they offer, and their approach to working with families.

During the initial consultation, caregivers should discuss their loved one's specific needs, preferences, and goals for care. A good palliative care team will focus on creating a personalized care plan that respects the individual's values and aligns with the family's expectations. Open communication and collaboration are key to ensuring that palliative care integrates seamlessly into the overall caregiving strategy.

Palliative care offers a compassionate and holistic approach to supporting individuals with dementia and their families, emphasizing comfort, dignity, and quality of life. By understanding its scope, determining eligibility, exploring its benefits, and finding the right providers, caregivers can navigate this stage of dementia care with confidence and reassurance.

Navigating Hospice Care: What Caregivers Need to Know

Hospice care represents a compassionate and holistic approach to end-of-life care, providing critical support for individuals with dementia and their families. As dementia progresses to its advanced stages, hospice care helps ensure that the individual's final months or weeks are as comfortable and dignified as possible. Understanding hospice care's philosophy, eligibility requirements, services, and family support can help caregivers navigate this sensitive phase with clarity and confidence.

Hospice care is centered on the philosophy of comfort, dignity, and quality of life. Unlike curative medical care, hospice focuses on relieving pain and managing symptoms rather than treating the underlying condition. The goal is to provide a peaceful and supportive environment, addressing the physical, emotional, and spiritual needs of the individual. Hospice care is not about giving up; rather, it's about ensuring that the individual receives the care they need to live their remaining time in the most meaningful and pain-free way possible. This approach also extends to families, offering resources and guidance to help them cope during this challenging period.

Eligibility for hospice care is determined by specific criteria, including a physician's certification that the individual's life expectancy is six months or less if the disease follows its natural course. For individuals with dementia, eligibility often includes factors such as severe cognitive decline, inability to perform basic activities of daily living (e.g., dressing, eating, or bathing), significant weight loss, and recurrent infections like pneumonia. While many families hesitate to initiate hospice care, waiting too long can mean missing out on valuable support and services. Hospice care can begin as soon as eligibility is met, allowing individuals and their families to benefit fully from the comprehensive care it provides.

The services offered by hospice care teams are designed to address all aspects of an individual's well-being. Medical support includes pain management, symptom relief, and assistance with medications or medical equipment. Skilled nurses and aides visit regularly to provide care, while on-call staff are available 24/7 for emergencies or urgent needs. Counseling services help address emotional and psychological challenges, providing comfort to both the individual and their caregivers. Spiritual care, often provided by chaplains or faith leaders, supports individuals in finding peace and meaning during their final stage of life. Additionally, hospice teams offer support for daily care tasks, such as bathing or repositioning, alleviating some of the caregiver's burden.

Families play a central role in hospice care, and the services provided extend to support them as well. Hospice care teams educate caregivers on how to manage symptoms, provide comfort, and navigate the practicalities of end-of-life care. Emotional support is a key component, with counselors and social workers available to help family members process their feelings and cope with the stress of caregiving. Bereavement support is also a hallmark of hospice care, continuing to assist families after their loved one's passing through grief counseling, support groups, and resources for navigating loss.

Caregivers should view hospice care as a partnership. Hospice professionals work collaboratively with families, respecting their input and incorporating their knowledge of the individual's preferences and needs. This teamwork ensures that care is personalized and aligned with the family's goals and values. Open communication with hospice staff fosters trust and helps address any concerns or questions that arise during this sensitive time.

For caregivers, choosing hospice care is a profound decision, but it is one that provides an invaluable network of support. Hospice care brings peace of mind, knowing that a team of dedicated professionals is focused on the comfort and dignity of their loved one. It also allows families to focus on meaningful moments and connections rather than the demands of caregiving alone.

Navigating hospice care is a journey of compassion, acceptance, and support. By understanding its philosophy, eligibility criteria, services, and family support, caregivers can make informed decisions that prioritize the well-being of both their loved one and themselves.

Legacy Planning and Memory Keeping

Legacy planning and memory keeping provide a meaningful way for caregivers and families to honor the lives of their loved ones with dementia, ensuring their stories, values, and impact endure across generations. These activities not only preserve cherished memories but also create opportunities for connection and reflection, even in the midst of caregiving challenges. By focusing on creating a lasting legacy, involving the individual with dementia, managing digital assets, and preserving important documents and memories, families can celebrate the essence of their loved one's life.

Creating a legacy begins with reflecting on what makes a loved one's life unique and meaningful. Memory books and photo albums are timeless ways to compile significant moments, milestones, and mementos. Video recordings can capture their voice, laughter, and personal reflections, adding a dynamic and emotional layer to the legacy. For families who wish to honor their loved one's impact on the community or a particular cause, establishing charitable contributions or scholarships in their name provides a way to extend their influence and keep their values alive. Other options include planting a tree, creating a custom piece of art, or compiling a family cookbook that preserves favorite recipes and stories behind them.

Involving the person with dementia in the process of legacy planning, when possible, adds depth and authenticity to the outcome. Engaging them in conversations about their favorite memories, values, and aspirations allows their voice to guide the legacy. Creative activities, such as scrapbooking, drawing, or storytelling, can encourage their participation in ways that align with their current abilities. For individuals in earlier stages of dementia, they may also wish to write letters, record messages, or share family traditions they hope to see carried forward. These contributions not only enhance the legacy but also provide moments of connection and joy in the present.

In today's digital age, managing a loved one's digital legacy is an important part of preserving their memory. This includes handling social media accounts, email addresses, and digital files. Caregivers should work with their loved one, if possible, to compile a list of passwords and instructions for managing these accounts. Many platforms, such as Facebook and Google, offer options for memorializing accounts or designating a trusted contact to handle them after a person's passing. This process ensures that digital assets are treated respectfully and remain accessible to the family as part of the overall legacy.

Preserving important documents and memories is another critical aspect of legacy planning. Legal documents, such as wills, advance directives, and property deeds, should be securely stored and easily accessible when needed. Photographs, letters, and other sentimental items can be digitized to ensure their longevity and to make sharing them with family members easier. Backing up digital files and organizing them into labeled folders provides clarity and security, ensuring that these treasures remain intact for future generations.

For caregivers, engaging in legacy planning and memory keeping offers more than a way to honor their loved one—it also provides a sense of purpose and a way to navigate the emotional complexities of caregiving. These acts of preservation affirm the enduring connection between caregiver and loved one, even as dementia alters the relationship. Sharing the completed legacy with extended family members fosters unity and provides a collective source of comfort and pride.

As caregivers conclude the practical and emotional preparations detailed in this chapter, it is important to reflect on their own journey. The role of caregiving transforms individuals, shaping them with resilience, compassion, and personal growth. In the next chapter we will explore how caregivers can process their experiences, embrace personal growth, and find closure as they move forward with their lives.

TEN

The Caregiver's Journey

Reflecting on the Caregiving Experience

The caregiving journey is one of profound transformation, marked by challenges, triumphs, and countless moments of connection. For those who have cared for a loved one with dementia, this experience leaves a lasting impact, shaping personal growth, resilience, and a deeper understanding of life. Reflecting on the journey allows caregivers to honor their efforts, recognize their strength, and find gratitude for the moments shared along the way. By acknowledging personal growth, celebrating challenges overcome, embracing gratitude, and reflecting on lessons learned, caregivers can close this chapter with a sense of fulfillment and purpose.

Caregiving fosters personal growth in ways that often remain unnoticed until the journey is complete. The relentless demands of caregiving teach resilience, patience, and adaptability, as caregivers learn to navigate ever-changing circumstances. Many caregivers emerge from this experience with a newfound sense of strength, having weathered moments of exhaustion, uncertainty, and grief. The journey also deepens empathy and compassion, as caregivers witness firsthand the vulnerabilities and strengths of their loved one. These qualities extend beyond caregiving, enriching relationships and interactions in other areas of life. Acknowledging this growth is an important step in embracing the person caregivers have become through their efforts.

Reflecting on the challenges faced and overcome emphasizes the extraordinary determination it took to provide care. From managing complex medical decisions and advocating for a loved one's needs to juggling personal responsibilities alongside caregiving, each hurdle represents a testament to the caregiver's commitment and courage. It's important to take pride in these accomplishments, recognizing that even in the face of setbacks or moments of doubt, the caregiver persevered with love and dedication. Celebrating these victories, big and small, helps caregivers recognize their own heroism in a journey that often goes unnoticed by others.

Amid the difficulties, caregiving offers moments of connection and joy that deserve to be cherished. Whether it's a smile sparked by a familiar song, a quiet moment of shared presence, or a laugh over a simple activity, these instances remind caregivers of the deep bond they share with their loved one. Finding gratitude for these moments provides a sense of balance, softening the weight of caregiving's challenges. Gratitude also allows caregivers to honor the relationship with their loved one, focusing on the love and humanity that defined their time together.

The caregiving journey is also a profound teacher, offering lessons that extend far beyond dementia care. Caregivers often gain insights into the importance of communication, patience, and presence. They learn the value of flexibility, the necessity of self-care, and the power of community. On a deeper level, caregiving teaches about the fragility and resilience of life, fostering an appreciation for the present moment and the connections that sustain us. Reflecting on these lessons helps caregivers integrate the experience into their own personal narratives, carrying forward the wisdom gained into future chapters of their lives.

As caregivers look back on their journey, it's natural to experience a mix of emotions—pride, relief, sadness, and even uncertainty about what comes next. It's important to honor these feelings and give space to process them. Caregivers should remind themselves that their efforts were not in vain, that their love and care provided comfort and dignity to their loved one. This reflection becomes a foundation for moving forward, allowing caregivers to celebrate the journey while embracing the possibilities that lie ahead.

The Importance of Community and Sharing Stories

Caregiving for a loved one with dementia is a journey often marked by emotional challenges and moments of isolation. However, it is also a journey that can be profoundly enriched by connection. Building a community of fellow caregivers and sharing experiences fosters understanding, support, and a collective sense of purpose. Through finding a tribe, sharing stories, and learning from others, caregivers can transform their individual experiences into a shared source of strength and advocacy.

Finding a community of fellow caregivers is one of the most impactful steps a caregiver can take to feel supported and understood. Whether through local support groups, online forums, or social organizations, connecting with others who have walked a similar path offers a sense of belonging that eases the isolation often associated with caregiving. These communities provide a safe space for caregivers to share their feelings, exchange practical advice, and simply be heard by people who truly understand. Fellow caregivers can empathize with the emotional highs and lows, offering encouragement and validation during difficult times. Joining a community fosters solidarity, reminding caregivers that they are not alone in their journey.

Sharing your story is a powerful way to contribute to this sense of connection while also creating a platform for advocacy and awareness. Whether through writing, speaking, or engaging on social media, sharing personal experiences allows caregivers to highlight the realities of dementia care and inspire others. Caregivers often find that expressing their stories helps them process their own emotions, celebrate the love they have given, and reflect on the journey they have traveled. Sharing also breaks down societal misconceptions about dementia, fostering greater understanding and compassion within the broader community.

The impact of sharing stories extends beyond personal catharsis; it can inspire change and support for other caregivers. By speaking openly about their experiences, caregivers can shine a light on the challenges and rewards of caregiving, encouraging others to seek help and build their own support networks. Stories can also serve as a call to action for improving resources, policies, and programs related to dementia care. Advocating for dementia awareness not only benefits others in similar situations but also honors the legacy of the loved ones who inspired the journey.

Equally valuable is the opportunity to learn from the experiences of others. Listening to fellow caregivers' stories provides practical insights and emotional reassurance. Each story offers a unique perspective, whether it's a solution to a caregiving challenge, a reflection on shared emotions, or a glimpse into how others have navigated difficult decisions. These lessons create a collective pool of wisdom that strengthens everyone within the community. Caregivers often describe moments of relief and connection when they hear someone else articulate the very feelings or struggles they have faced, fostering mutual empathy and understanding.

Engaging with a caregiving community also encourages the exchange of strategies and resources. Caregivers can learn about useful tools, financial assistance programs, or innovative approaches to managing behavioral symptoms. Beyond practical advice, the stories of others can inspire hope and resilience, showing that joy and connection are possible even amidst the complexities of caregiving.

As caregivers build connections, they contribute to a broader movement that elevates the role of caregiving in society. The collective voices of caregivers can influence how communities and institutions address the needs of those affected by dementia. Advocacy efforts, whether through fundraising, awareness campaigns, or policy initiatives, gain strength through the shared experiences of those who understand caregiving firsthand.

The importance of community and storytelling lies in their ability to transform caregiving from a solitary effort into a shared journey of resilience, compassion, and purpose. By finding a tribe, sharing their stories, and learning from others, caregivers can enrich their own experiences while contributing to a stronger, more supportive world for dementia care.

Transitioning from Caregiver to Advocate

The end of an active caregiving journey often leaves caregivers with a profound sense of purpose and a deep well of experience. While the day-to-day responsibilities may lessen, the lessons learned and the connection to dementia care remain. Transitioning from caregiver to advocate allows individuals to channel their experiences into meaningful action, advocating for better care, raising awareness, and driving change. By leveraging their experiences, exploring advocacy opportunities, and continuing to fight for improvements in dementia care, former caregivers can leave a lasting impact on their communities and the lives of others.

The caregiving journey provides a unique perspective that positions former caregivers as powerful advocates for change. Drawing on firsthand experiences, they can highlight the challenges and gaps in dementia care, from the need for improved support systems to greater access to resources. Advocacy begins with sharing stories and insights, whether through public speaking engagements, community forums, or written pieces. These personal narratives resonate with others, humanizing the struggles and triumphs of dementia care and inspiring both empathy and action. Policymakers, healthcare providers, and organizations often respond more strongly to stories that illuminate real-world implications, making former caregivers an invaluable voice in shaping better systems.

Volunteer and advocacy opportunities offer tangible ways to make an impact. Many organizations dedicated to dementia care and research actively seek volunteers to participate in awareness campaigns, fundraising events, or support groups. Groups like the Alzheimer's Association or similar local organizations provide avenues to contribute time and expertise. Volunteering at memory care facilities or adult day programs can also be a way to stay connected to the dementia community while providing meaningful contributions.

Becoming involved in advocacy groups focused on dementia offers additional platforms for driving change. These groups often engage in efforts to influence legislation, promote funding for dementia research, and improve caregiver resources. Former caregivers can play key roles in these initiatives by sharing their experiences, participating in public campaigns, or working directly with decision-makers. Advocacy opportunities may include testifying before legislative committees, participating in rallies, or joining advisory boards focused on dementia care policies.

Continuing the fight for awareness and change goes beyond formal advocacy efforts. Former caregivers can lead by example in their communities, educating friends, family, and colleagues about the realities of dementia care and the importance of understanding and support. Simple actions, like organizing informational events, starting conversations on social media, or hosting support group meetings, can create ripples of awareness that extend far beyond immediate circles.

Even after the personal caregiving journey ends, staying involved in the fight for better dementia care provides a sense of ongoing purpose and connection. Advocating for funding, innovation, and education in dementia research ensures that progress continues for future generations of caregivers and individuals living with dementia. Whether contributing to research initiatives, participating in clinical trials, or raising funds for related causes, every effort supports the advancement of knowledge and resources that can ease the burden on future families.

For many former caregivers, advocacy also serves as a way to honor their loved one's memory. By dedicating time and energy to improving dementia care, they ensure that their loved one's legacy contributes to a broader impact. Advocacy becomes a means of preserving the love and dedication that defined their caregiving journey, transforming personal experiences into a force for positive change.

Transitioning from caregiver to advocate is a natural progression for those who wish to extend the meaning of their caregiving journey. By leveraging their experience, exploring volunteer and advocacy opportunities, and remaining committed to raising awareness and driving change, former caregivers contribute to a world that better understands, supports, and cares for those affected by dementia.

Finding Closure and Moving Forward

The conclusion of a caregiving journey often brings a profound mix of emotions—grief, relief, and uncertainty about what lies ahead. After dedicating so much time and energy to supporting a loved one with dementia, caregivers may find themselves struggling to redefine their identity and purpose. Finding closure and moving forward involves processing grief, rediscovering oneself, embracing new beginnings, and honoring the caregiving journey. By taking these steps, caregivers can transition to a new chapter of life while preserving the meaning and love that defined their caregiving experience.

Processing grief is a deeply personal and nonlinear process, particularly when the loss is preceded by years of gradual change and anticipatory grief. The loss of a loved one with dementia often feels layered—caregivers grieve not only the passing of their loved one but also the gradual loss of the person they knew before the disease took hold. Healthy grieving requires allowing oneself to feel the full spectrum of emotions without judgment. Sadness, anger, guilt, and relief are all natural responses to loss. Seeking support through grief counseling, support groups, or trusted friends and family members provides an outlet for these emotions and reinforces that no one has to grieve alone. Expressing feelings through journaling, art, or other creative outlets can also help process grief in a constructive way.

Rediscovering self after caregiving is a vital step in moving forward. The caregiving role often becomes all-encompassing, leaving little time for personal interests or aspirations. With this chapter of life behind them, caregivers have an opportunity to explore who they are beyond their role as a caregiver. Revisiting old hobbies, taking up new activities, or pursuing educational or career goals can reignite a sense of purpose and fulfillment. Reflection is key during this phase —asking questions like, "What brings me joy?" or "What have I always wanted to try?" helps caregivers reconnect with their passions and redefine their identity.

New beginnings come in many forms and offer a chance to embrace the possibilities ahead. Some caregivers find joy in building new relationships, whether through friendships, romantic partnerships, or deeper connections within their existing networks. Others may choose to dedicate themselves to causes they're passionate about, such as volunteering, advocacy, or creative pursuits. This phase is also an opportunity to invest in personal well-being by prioritizing health, mindfulness, and self-care. It's important to approach new beginnings with an open heart and patience, recognizing that transitions take time and every step forward is meaningful.

Honoring the caregiving journey is an essential part of finding closure. The time, effort, and love poured into caring for a loved one with dementia are acts of deep devotion that deserve recognition. Reflecting on this journey allows caregivers to see the strength and resilience they demonstrated, as well as the impact they had on their loved one's quality of life. Memorializing the journey through a written tribute, photo album, or even a small ceremony provides a way to celebrate the shared love and the legacy created together. Acknowledging the challenges faced and the lessons learned honors not only the caregiver's effort but also the person they cared for.

As caregivers move forward, they carry with them the growth, empathy, and perspective gained from their experiences. The caregiving journey, though difficult, leaves an indelible mark that shapes how they approach the world and the people in it. Closure does not mean forgetting or moving on from the loved one they cared for—it means finding peace in the knowledge that they did their best and that their loved one's memory will continue to live in their actions and choices.

Moving forward after caregiving is a deeply personal process, filled with both challenges and opportunities. By processing grief, rediscovering identity, embracing new beginnings, and honoring the caregiving journey, former caregivers can create a fulfilling new chapter while cherishing the love and memories that shaped their past.

Resources and Next Steps for Dementia Caregivers

The transition to a new phase of life often comes with questions about what comes next. Whether it involves continuing to support the dementia caregiving community, prioritizing personal growth, or planning for one's own future, the resources available can be invaluable. By leveraging a comprehensive resource list, continuing education opportunities, self-care tools, and future planning guidance, caregivers can find support, empowerment, and clarity for the road ahead.

A comprehensive resource list equips caregivers with tools to address a wide range of needs, from practical caregiving advice to emotional support. Organizations like the Alzheimer's Association, Dementia Alliance International, and the Family Caregiver Alliance offer robust resources, including hotlines, informational guides, and local support groups. Websites such as Help for Alzheimer's Families or the National Institute on Aging provide reliable information about dementia progression, treatment, and care techniques. Books like *The 36-Hour Day* by Nancy L. Mace and Peter V. Rabins, or *Creating Moments of Joy Along the Alzheimer's Journey* by Jolene Brackey, offer practical insights and uplifting perspectives. Online forums and social media groups also create spaces where caregivers can connect, share experiences, and seek advice.

Continued education is another vital step for caregivers who wish to deepen their knowledge or prepare for potential future caregiving roles. Workshops, seminars, and online courses provide opportunities to stay informed about advancements in dementia care and related fields. Platforms like Coursera or edX offer courses on topics such as dementia care, communication techniques, and elder law, while local universities and community organizations frequently host in-person training sessions. Continuing education not only enhances caregiving skills but also empowers individuals to advocate for better dementia care in their communities.

Self-care resources are essential for caregivers to maintain their mental and emotional well-being. Apps like Calm or Headspace offer guided meditation and relaxation techniques tailored to stress reduction. Online therapy platforms, such as BetterHelp or Talkspace, connect caregivers with mental health professionals for ongoing support. Caregivers should also explore local yoga studios, fitness classes, or wellness retreats that prioritize mental and physical health. Many caregiver-focused organizations, like Well Spouse Association, offer programs specifically designed to support the caregiver's emotional journey, providing a safe space to share feelings and experiences.

Planning for the future is an opportunity for caregivers to prioritize their own well-being and legacy. Just as they have planned for their loved one's needs, caregivers should consider their own healthcare, legal, and financial plans. Reviewing health insurance policies, exploring long-term care insurance, and creating advance directives ensure that their future needs are met. Financial planning, including budgeting for retirement and estate planning, offers security and peace of mind. Working with professionals such as financial advisors or elder law attorneys can simplify these processes and provide personalized guidance.

Legacy planning is also a meaningful step for caregivers looking to reflect on their journey and the impact they wish to leave behind. This might involve creating a memoir, starting a blog, or participating in advocacy work to improve resources and awareness for dementia care. Charitable contributions, such as donating to dementia research organizations or establishing a scholarship in a loved one's name, ensure that their caregiving legacy continues to make a difference.

As caregivers transition into their next phase of life, the support and resources available to them create opportunities for growth, healing, and empowerment. By staying connected to a community of caregivers, prioritizing self-care, continuing education, and preparing for the future, they can navigate this new chapter with confidence and purpose.

Conclusion

The caregiving journey is an emotional and practical rollercoaster, filled with challenges, unexpected moments of joy, and profound personal growth. Dementia caregiving requires patience, resilience, and strength, as caregivers navigate the ever-changing landscape of the disease while balancing the needs of their loved ones with their own well-being. Despite the difficulties, this journey is deeply meaningful, offering caregivers the opportunity to forge unbreakable bonds and create cherished memories with their loved ones. The courage and dedication demonstrated throughout this experience are a testament to the remarkable strength within every caregiver.

This book has aimed to serve as a comprehensive guide for caregivers, offering tools and strategies to navigate the complexities of dementia care. From understanding the nature of dementia and developing practical caregiving techniques to managing the emotional toll and addressing legal and financial challenges, the book has covered the critical aspects of this journey. Key takeaways include the importance of self-care, building a robust support network, and maintaining a connection with your loved one even as their cognitive abilities change. Preparing for advanced care and planning for the future ensures that both the individual with dementia and their caregivers face fewer uncertainties.

Now, as you close this chapter of the book, consider how your own experiences can contribute to a broader cause. Advocacy is a powerful way to transform personal challenges into collective progress. By sharing your story, whether through writing, public speaking, or informal conversations, you can illuminate the path for others navigating similar journeys. Your voice has the potential to foster a more informed and compassionate society regarding dementia care, inspire improvements in resources, and provide encouragement to other caregivers.

It's important to acknowledge that, for many, the caregiving journey continues beyond the pages of this book. While the challenges of dementia caregiving are ongoing, so too are the opportunities for connection, growth, and meaningful moments. You are not alone in this experience—there is a community of caregivers, advocates, and professionals ready to support you. The lessons and tools you've gained throughout this book, combined with the strength you've cultivated through your journey, will guide you as you move forward.

Finding and participating in support networks is one of the most valuable actions you can take. Whether through local groups, online forums, or national organizations, connecting with others who share your experiences fosters understanding and solidarity. Shared stories and insights provide both practical solutions and emotional comfort, reinforcing that no one needs to face the challenges of caregiving alone.

Equally important is the need to prioritize self-care. Caregivers often place their loved ones' needs above their own, but sustained caregiving requires a foundation of personal well-being. Revisit the self-care strategies outlined in this book, and remain open to exploring new ones. Your health and happiness are essential—not only for your own sake but also for the quality of care you can provide to others.

To further support your journey, a curated list of resources is provided, including websites, hotlines, books, and tools that address a wide range of caregiver needs. These resources span emotional support, practical advice on caregiving, and guidance on legal and financial matters, offering continued learning and assistance at every stage.

As you consider your next steps, think about your own future planning. Health, legal, and financial preparedness are essential for your peace of mind and security. Just as you have planned for the needs of your loved one, now is the time to ensure that your own plans are in place, creating a legacy and a roadmap for your well-being.

Closing this book, reflect on the incredible difference you have made in the life of your loved one. Your efforts, sacrifices, and love have provided comfort and dignity in the face of a difficult journey. This caregiving experience has not only shaped you but also created a lasting impact on those around you. Carry forward the hope, resilience, and wisdom you have gained, knowing that you are part of a larger community dedicated to making the world a better place for those living with dementia and their caregivers. You are not alone—and your journey matters.

Sharing the Journey

"To care for those who once cared for us is one of life's greatest honors." – Tia Walker

Thank you for joining me on this journey through the challenges and rewards of dementia caregiving. I hope the insights and strategies shared in this book have given you clarity and confidence as you care for your loved one. But the journey doesn't end here—your experience and voice can help others who are just beginning to navigate this path.

Your review on Amazon is more than just feedback—it's an opportunity to guide other caregivers toward resources that can ease their burden and offer valuable support. By sharing your thoughts, you're helping others gain the knowledge and encouragement they need to approach caregiving with confidence and compassion.

Scan this QR code to leave your review on Amazon.

Every caregiver's journey is unique, but we all benefit from hearing each other's stories and perspectives. Your review can be a powerful way to connect with others, reassure them that they're not alone, and show them the tools and guidance available to make caregiving more manageable.

Thank you for being part of this effort. Your insights and experiences matter, and your willingness to share them is appreciated more than you know. Together, we can help create a stronger, more informed community of caregivers.

With deep gratitude,

Vivian Hart

www.ingramcontent.com/pod-product-compliance
Lightning Source LLC
Chambersburg PA
CBHW072006150726
47999CB00002B/532